A publication of the
**National Wildfire
Coordinating Group**

Interagency
Aerial Supervision
Guide

PMS 505

April 2013

NFES 002544

Interagency Aerial Supervision Guide

April 2013
PMS 505
NFES 002544

Sponsored for NWCG publication by the NWCG National Interagency Aviation Committee. Questions regarding the content of this product should be directed to the National Interagency Aviation Committee members listed at http://www.nwcg.gov/branches/et/niac/index.htm. Revisions and corrections to this guide should be directed to Gil Dustin at gil_dustin@blm.gov. Questions and comments may also be emailed to BLM_FA_NWCG_Products@blm.gov.

This product is available electronically at: http://www.nwcg.gov. Printed copies may be ordered from the Great Basin Cache, National Interagency Fire Center, Boise, ID. For ordering procedures and costs, please refer to the annual *NFES Catalog Part 2: Publications* posted at http://www.nwcg.gov/pms/pubs/catalog.htm.

Previous editions: 2011.

Table of Contents

Figures

Tables

Additional reference items are located on NIFC's aviation Web page at
http://www.blm.gov/nifc/st/en/prog/fire/Aviation/aerial_supervision.html

Task Books

Aviation Guides

Leadplane Information

Tanker Base Maps

Radio Programming

Aerial Supervision Forms

Checklists

Crew Resource Management

Tools

This page intentionally left blank.

Chapter 1 – Introduction

1) Goal

To promote safe, effective, and efficient aerial supervision services in support of incident goals and objectives.

2) Objectives

Consolidate the *Interagency Leadplane Guide*, *Aerial Supervision Module Guide*, and the *Interagency Air Tactical Group Supervisors Guide* into one document which will:

a)   State consistent interagency aerial supervision standards and procedures.

b)   Define the roles, responsibilities, and scope of each aerial supervision position.

c)   Enhance information sharing between Air Tactical Group Supervisors (ATGS), Aerial Supervision Modules (ASM), Leadplane Pilots, Airtanker Coordinators (ATCO), Air Tactical Pilots (ATP), Air Tactical Supervisors (ATS), and Helicopter Coordinators (HLCO).

d)   Provide a common interagency guide, which can be utilized by all members of the aerial supervision community.

3) Scope

This *Interagency Aerial Supervision Guide* is to be used by federal and participating state or local agencies in the accomplishment of the numerous aerial supervision roles as defined by the United States Incident Command System (ICS).

4) Authority

The Interagency Aerial Supervision Subcommittee (IASS) is responsible for the update and completion of this guide with oversight provided by the National Interagency Aviation Committee (NIAC). The National Wildfire Coordinating Group (NWCG) provides the authority to develop this guide.

5) Publication Mechanism

The *Interagency Aerial Supervision Guide*, PMS 505, is available electronically from the NWCG Web site at http://www.nwcg.gov and printed copies are available through the cache system. The *Interagency Aerial Supervision Log Book*, PMS 509, is also available electronically from the NWCG Web site. Supplemental information is available online from the BLM aviation site at http://www.aviation.blm.gov.

6) Review and Revision Schedule

IASS will review the *Interagency Aerial Supervision Guide* on an annual basis. Revisions to the guide will be made and disseminated annually to reflect significant changes in interagency policy and procedures as they affect aerial supervision operations. The *Aerial Supervision Logbook* is on a 3-year revision.

The following chart depicts the current national aerial supervision management structure.

Figure 1. National Aerial Supervision Management Structure (2013)

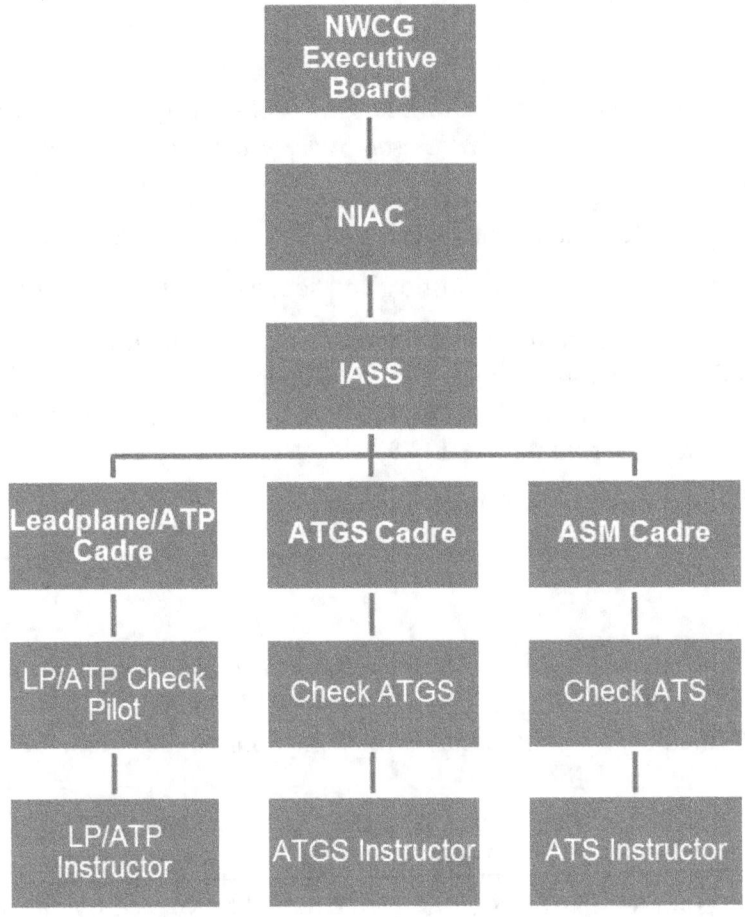

Acronyms: NWCG – National Wildfire Coordinating Group

NIAC – National Interagency Aviation Committee

IASS – Interagency Aerial Supervision Subcommittee

ATS – Air Tactical Supervisor

ATP – Air Tactical Pilot

ASM – Aerial Supervision Module

ATGS – Air Tactical Group Supervisor

Chapter 2 – Aerial Supervision Roles and Responsibilities

There are five types of aerial supervision resources and six aerial supervisor classifications. Although these positions are unique, they share the common purpose of facilitating safe, effective, and efficient air operations in support of incident objectives.

1) Air Tactical Group Supervisor (ATGS)

The ATGS coordinates incident airspace and manages incident air traffic. The ATGS is an airborne firefighter who coordinates, assigns, and evaluates the use of aerial resources in support of incident objectives. The ATGS is the link between ground personnel and incident aircraft. The ATGS must collaborate with ground personnel to develop and implement tactical and logistical missions on an incident. The ATGS must be proactive in communicating current and expected fire and weather conditions. The ATGS must provide candid feedback regarding the effectiveness of aviation operations and overall progress toward meeting incident objectives. The ATGS must also work with dispatch staff to coordinate the ordering, assignment, and release of incident aircraft in accordance with the needs of fire management and incident command personnel.

On initial attack incidents (type 4 and 5), the ATGS will size-up, prioritize, and coordinate the response of aerial and ground resources until a qualified Incident Commander (IC) arrives. On complex incidents (type 1, 2, or 3), the ATGS will coordinate and prioritize the use of aircraft between several divisions/groups while maintaining communications with operations personnel and aircraft bases (fixed/rotor).

In the Incident Command System (ICS), the ATGS works for the IC on initial attack and the Operations Section Chief (OSC), Air Operations Branch Director (AOBD), or operational designee on extended attack. The ATGS supervises the ATCO, Leadplane Pilot, and the HLCO positions when activated. The ATGS is qualified to function as an ATCO or HLCO.

2) Airtanker Coordinator (ATCO)

The ATCO coordinates, directs, and evaluates airtanker operations. The ATCO works under the ATGS. This position is typically activated on complex incidents where several airtankers are assigned. An ATCO can reduce the span of control of the ATGS by managing all the airtankers over an incident. If no ATGS is present, the ATCO works for the IC. **The ATCO is not authorized for low level (below 500' AGL) operations.**

3) Leadplane Pilot (Lead)

The Leadplane position is identical to the ATCO except the pilot is qualified and authorized for low level operations. A Leadplane Pilot is not recognized in ICS and is classified as an ATCO by default. The low level capabilities of a Leadplane enhance the safety and effectiveness of airtanker operations in the often turbulent, smoky, and congested fire environment.

4) Helicopter Coordinator (HLCO)

The HLCO coordinates, directs, and evaluates tactical/logistical helicopter operations. The HLCO position is typically activated on complex incidents where several helicopters are assigned. A HLCO can reduce the span of control of the ATGS by managing all the helicopters over an incident. The HLCO may provide sole aerial supervision on an incident where only helicopters are assigned, otherwise ATGS is required. When an ATGS is assigned, the HLCO is a subordinate position to the ATGS. If no ATGS is present, the HLCO works for the IC, AOBD, or designee.

Other than the pre-requisite requirements for ATGS, HLCO organizational structure, currency, and refresher requirements are recommended to mirror the ATGS program.

5) Aerial Supervision Module (ASM)

An ASM is a two person crew functioning as the Lead and ATGS from the same aircraft. The ASM crew is qualified in their respective positions and has received additional training and authorization. An ASM can be utilized as a Lead, ATGS, or both, depending on the needs of incident management personnel. An ASM consists of an Air Tactical Pilot and Air Tactical Supervisor.

e) Air Tactical Pilot (ATP) – The ATP is a qualified Leadplane Pilot who has received specialized training and authorization to function as an ASM crewmember. The ATP functions as the Leadplane pilot and utilizes Crew Resource Management (CRM) skills to evaluate and share the incident workload with the ATS.

f) Air Tactical Supervisor (ATS) – The ATS is a qualified ATGS who has received specialized training and authorization to function as an ASM crewmember. The ATS is an ATGS who also utilizes CRM to evaluate and share the incident workload with the ATP.

The following charts depict the relation of Aerial Supervision to other resources in ICS.

Figure 2. Aerial Supervision in Extended Attack and Initial Attack

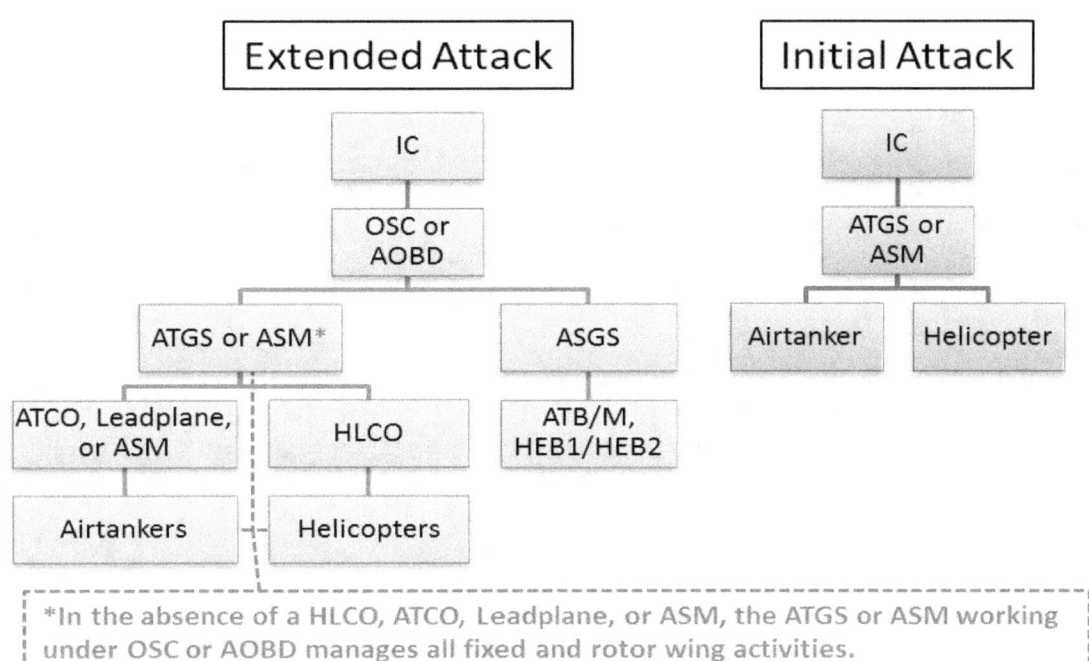

This page intentionally left blank.

Chapter 3 – Administration, Training, Certification, and Currency

The policies governing each functional area of aerial supervision are unique. As such, these areas have different standards for program management, qualification, training, certification, and currency.

The *Wildland Fire Qualification System Guide* (PMS 310-1) will be revised in the fall of 2013 to reflect changes to the ATGS initial qualification and refresher training requirements, which will be effective in 2014. Federal and CALFIRE mission requirements have changed and are in effect for 2013.

1) Air Tactical Group Supervisor (ATGS)

a) Introduction

This section describes the qualifications, training, certification, and currency requirements necessary to perform as an ATGS.

Program administration is assigned at the national and geographic area level. Agency identified fire and aviation managers are responsible for the ATGS program direction, management and general program safety standards.

Aerial supervision operations place a high demand on communication and management skills. Application of fire behavior knowledge combined with ground fire resource capability must be correlated with tactical aircraft mission planning to safely and effectively utilize aircraft to support incident management objectives.

b) Administration

Interagency standards for ATGS operations are developed by the Interagency Aerial Supervision Subcommittee (IASS), a sub-group of the National Interagency Aviation Committee (NIAC). The following positions have been identified by the IASS to manage the air attack program at regional, state, and local levels.

i) **National and State ATGS Program Managers** – Aviation management specialists designated by their respective agencies. These positions are responsible to administer the ATGS program at either a national or state level. Roles and responsibilities of this position include:

(1) Coordinate with the ATGS Cadre Chair to provide program coordination on an interagency basis for participating federal, state, and local agencies.

(2) Coordinate with the ATGS Cadre Chair to maintain and update a national database containing pertinent information regarding qualified and trainee ATGS personnel, ATGS Cadre members, ATGS Instructors (ATGS I), and Check ATGS (ATGS C).

(3) Ensure agency ATGS currency requirements are met by annually reviewing ATGS mission summaries.

(4) Coordinate with agencies that have or desire to develop an ATGS program.

(5) Act in the capacity as program liaison with other interagency groups including the ASM Cadre, Leadplane Cadre, Interagency Helicopter Operations Program Steering Committee (IHOPS), the Interagency SEAT Steering Committee (ISSC), the Interagency Airspace Steering Committee (IASC), and the Smokejumper community.

(6) Coordinate with the ATGS Cadre Chair to ensure the development and maintenance of an interagency cadre of qualified ATGS I and ATGS C.

(7) Coordinate with the ATGS Cadre Chair to maintain interagency ATGS currency and standardization training at the geographic area level.

(8) Coordinate mission evaluation requirements with international cooperators (Canada) for American ATGS operating under international agreements.

(9) Provide input to the annual revision of the *Interagency Aerial Supervision Guide* and ensure distribution of program related information updates to ATGS Cadre members.

ii) **ATGS Cadre** - A sub-group of IASS who either Geographic Area or state ATGS Program Managers and administer the ATGS program at the geographic area level on an interagency basis. Roles and responsibilities of this position include:

(1) Serve as the point of contact to the ATGS Cadre Chair for the ATGS program within the designated GACC.

(2) Serve as the lead ATGS C in the respective GACC.

(3) Coordinate a training and currency program for qualified ATGS and trainees on an interagency basis at the geographic area level.

(4) Coordinate geographic area level mentoring for ATGS trainees.

(5) Make recommendations concerning training priorities to the ATGS Cadre Chair, interagency aviation managers and geographic area coordination centers.

(6) Coordinate the ATGS program with other aviation programs at the geographic area level.

(7) Develop, coordinate and conduct initial and currency training programs within the geographic area.

(8) Gather ATGS annual mission summaries and refresher training attendance for ATGS within the designated GACC. Forward annual documentation to agency program managers, and fire qualifications managers as necessary.

(9) Function in the capacity of ATGS C and ATGS I.

(10) Provide program and technical assistance as required to interagency user groups and partners.

(11) Disseminate ATGS related program and technical information to user groups at the geographic area level.

(12) Position Requirements:

    (a) One year of ATGS C experience.

    (b) Possess experience in the position of ATGS in multiple geographic areas, fuel models and incident complexity.

    (c) Maintain currency as an ATGS I and C.

    (d) Retired individuals are not authorized to perform in this position unless authorized through the GACC ATGS Cadre.

iii) **Check ATGS (ATGS C)** Individuals authorized at the GACC level by the ATGS Cadre that provide mission evaluations.

(1) Roles and responsibilities:

    (a) Evaluate the performance of individuals seeking to become certified as ATGS.

    (b) Provide mission evaluations for individuals currently certified as ATGS to ensure performance meets the interagency standard.

    (c) Provide written documentation of ATGS/ATGS (T) performance to the ATGS Cadre member or interagency aviation managers along with recommendations for additional training or retention of the individual as an ATGS as appropriate.

    (d) The ATGS Cadre will certify and track ATGS (C).

(2) Position Requirements:

    (a) 1 year of ATGS (I) qualification.

    (b) Pass an evaluation flight performed by an ATGS (C).

    (c) The ATGS Cadre chair will issue a certificate of evaluation flight completion, which will be forwarded to the supervisor/IQCS Manager.

    (d) Currency requirement: Same as ATGS.

(e) Retired individuals are not authorized to perform in this position unless approved by the ATGS Cadre or agency program manager.

iv) **ATGS Instructor (ATGS I)** – Individuals authorized at the GACC level by either the ATGS Cadre or the individuals program manager that provide instruction in the capacity as a trainer/instructor on ATGS mission flights. Roles and responsibilities of this position include evaluating trainee performance through completion of Aerial Supervision Mission Evaluation forms.

    (1) Position Requirements:

        (a) 1 Year following ATGS qualification.

        (b) Pass an evaluation flight performed by an ATGS (C).

        (c) The ATGS Cadre chair will issue a certificate of evaluation flight completion, which will be forwarded to the supervisor/IQCS Manager.

        (d) Retired individuals are authorized for this position providing they meet the position requirements.

        (e) Currency requirement: Same as ATGS.

        (f) The ATGS Cadre will certify and track ATGS (I).

c) Initial ATGS Training and Certification

Candidates will meet or exceed prerequisite experience requirements and mandatory training requirements listed in the PMS 310-1.

i) **Classroom Training** – S-378, Aerial Supervision or CAL FIRE C-378, Aerial Supervision

ii) **Agency Approved CRM Training (effective 2014)**

iii) **Flight Training Requirements** – Prior to initial certification, ATGS candidates should have a variety of on-the-job training. The following flight training requirements provide guidance for evaluating ATGS candidates. Individualized training and evaluation programs should be developed to refine the skills and abilities of each trainee prior to certification. Each flight training program should include a variety of work experience and be of sufficient duration to ensure that the individual can independently function in the position of air tactical group supervisor following initial certification.

    (1) Observing an ATGS (I) during ongoing incident operations: Candidates should observe a qualified ATGS for a minimum of three missions prior to undertaking on-the-job training assignments under the supervision of an ATGS (I).

    (2) On-the-job training under the direct supervision of an ATGS (I).

(a) Prior to initial certification, candidates should undertake an on-the-job training program under the supervision of an ATGS (I) that provides a variety of experience in initial and extended attack scenarios.

(b) A minimum of 10 missions (mission - see glossary) under the direct supervision of an ATGS (I) is recommended to ensure the candidate is capable of satisfactorily functioning in the capacity as ATGS in a variety of settings, incident complexities and fuel models.

(3) **ATGS Candidate Evaluations** – The candidate should receive a written evaluation at the completion of each mission from the ATGS (I) as an integral part of the mission de-briefing. The Aerial Supervision Mission Evaluation is the standard performance assessment tool. The candidate will retain a copy of the mission evaluation to supplement information completed by the ATGS (I) in the candidate's task book.

(4) **ATGS Training Opportunities** – ATGS Cadre Members can assist in the development of candidates by assigning a mentor and providing a variety of training opportunities in different locales, fuel types and incident complexities. Training opportunities may include the following:

(a) Assignments to work with full-time, dedicated/exclusive use ATGS at an air attack base.

(b) Assignments to a national or geographic area Incident Management Team (IMT).

(c) Details or training assignments in other geographic areas to increase the depth of experience.

(d) Participate as a passenger on other tactical aircraft during tactical missions (subject to approval from the National Program Manager, Contracting Officer, Contractor and Pilot in Command).

d) **ATGS Certification Process**

The ATGS task book must be completed within three years of the initiation date as required by PMS 310-1. Upon completion of the task book, the designated GACC ATGS Cadre member/agency ATGS Coordinator will:

i) Coordinate a final mission evaluation with an ATGS (C).

ii) Upon completion of the final mission evaluation, the ATGS (C) will return the completed task book to the certifying official along with the appropriate recommendations completed.

These added steps in the initial certification process are intended to ensure the candidate has received a variety of training assignments that represent a cross section of incident complexities, and the candidate is proficient to undertake the responsibilities of the position.

e)   Supplemental ATGS Training

The following training opportunities should be considered prior to initial certification or as supplemental or refresher training individuals currently certified as air tactical group supervisors:

i)   Pinch Hitter pilot course

ii)   Private pilot ground school

iii)   National Aerial Fire Fighting Academy (NAFA)

The GACC Cadre member or agency training official can assist in the development of candidates by providing a variety of training opportunities in different locales, fuel types and incident complexities. Training opportunities may include the following:

i)   Assignments to work with full-time, dedicated, or exclusive use ATGS at an air attack base.

ii)   Assignments to a national or geographic area IMT.

Related aviation training opportunities should be made available to candidates to provide valuable knowledge, experience and skills applicable to the ATGS position including:

i)   Participation in aerial reconnaissance or aerial detection missions.

ii)   Observing or participating in large helibase operations.

iii)   Orientation to airtanker base and retardant operations.

iv)   Orientation to or observation of aircraft dispatch operations.

f)   ATGS Currency Requirements (effective immediately)

All ATGS will meet the requirements stated in the PMS 310-1. **In addition, all federal agency and federal agency sponsored ATGS will**:

i)   **Annually** perform, document, and report a minimum of 5 missions[1].

ii)   **Annually** forward an annual mission summary[2] to the appropriate GACC ATGS Cadre member (feds) or agency program manager.

CALFIRE supports the above currency requirements and manages them internally.

Failure to meet the currency requirements will revert the ATGS to trainee status in IQCS. The ATGS will require local recurrency training, which will address the required elements of RT-378 (next page) and will include the moderate complexity (a mix of at least 4 fixed and rotor wing aircraft) flight/STEX exercise (See refresher training – RT-378). This training will serve to recertify an ATGS whose currency has lapsed.

A certificate (or agency record of completion) will be issued by the instructor and forwarded to the GACC ATGS Cadre member (or agency program manager) and the appropriate IQCS or qualification management official.

[1] The GACC ATGS Cadre member (feds) and agency program manager (CALFIRE) will track annual missions and report mission currency lapses to the appropriate IQCS or qualification management official and the national program manager (feds).

[2] Annual Mission Summaries, Individual Mission forms, and Mission Evaluation forms are components of the Aerial Supervision Log Book (NFES 1150).

g) **ATGS Refresher Training (RT-378)**

All ATGS are required to attend and pass RT-378 triennially (effective 2014).

Beginning in 2014, an ATGS refresher/recertification training will be conducted at a minimum of every three years at the local, geographic or national level and will include the following components. This training will serve to recertify an ATGS whose currency has lapsed.

Proficiency Exercise: All ATGS will demonstrate proficiency in the required refresher elements and complete a moderate complexity (a mix of at least 4 fixed and rotor wing aircraft) mission or flight/STEX exercise (appendix C). The exercise will represent a typical IA and will require the ATGS to demonstrate the minimum acceptable skill set of the position including FTA entry, determining FTA altitudes, initial aircraft briefings, aircraft separation, communication with air and ground resources, and situational awareness.

Performance will be documented on a Mission Evaluation, reviewed with the participant, and forwarded to the GACC ATGS Cadre Member or appropriate agency official. Failure to demonstrate an acceptable level of proficiency will require the ATGS performance deficiency or decertification process to be implemented.

Required refresher elements:

i) Proficiency exercise

ii) Risk management

iii) Mission procedures

iv) FTA management

v) Agency approved CRM refresher

Optional Elements

i) Radio programming

ii) Map reading and navigation

iii) Fire and aviation weather

iv) Strategy and tactics

v) Aviation incidents/accidents from the preceding season

vi) Payment documents

vii) Contract and aircraft fleet updates

viii) Issues and concerns from national and/or regional user groups (fire management, dispatch, hotshots, incident commanders, etc.)

A certificate of completion (or agency record of completion) will be issued to attendees who pass and it will be forwarded to the GACC ATGS Cadre member or appropriate agency official and the IQCS/IQS official.

h) **ATGS Mission Evaluation**

The standard method for evaluating ATGS performance is an actual or simulated mission utilizing the ATGS Mission Evaluation form.

Mission Evaluations are conducted by ATGS (I/C) for the following reasons:

i) ATGS training

ii) ATGS certification

iii) ATGS currency

iv) ATGS performance deficiencies (next page)

i) **ATGS Performance Deficiencies and Decertification**

If an ATGS is observed performing unsafely/deficiently:

i) The event will be discussed with the individual, and if needed, documented on a Mission Evaluation, performance evaluation, unit log, or other agency appropriate form.

ii) Depending on the agency, the documentation will be forwarded to the GACC ATGS Cadre member or the agency program manager, and the individual's supervisor or sponsoring agency/official.

iii) The individual will be made unavailable for ATGS assignments in the appropriate dispatch/status system.

iv) The agency program manager or the individual's supervisor or sponsoring agency official will implement the following alternative courses of action:

(1) Clarify the performance standards and the consequences of not meeting them.

(2) Conduct or schedule a mission evaluation performed on an actual incident of minimally moderate complexity (a mix of at least 4 fixed and rotor wing aircraft).

(3) If needed, recommend the qualification be removed via the appropriate IQCS or agency official.

v) If the evaluation flight option is selected, the following outcomes are possible with **approval of the individuals supervisor.**

(1) Pass evaluation flight and return to available status in the appropriate dispatch/status system.

(2) Fail the evaluation flight and be returned to ATGS (T) status and receive remedial ATGS training.

(3) Fail the evaluation flight and have qualification removed by the supervisor/IQCS official.

2) Leadplane Pilot

The term "Leadplane Pilot" is used by the USDA (USFS) and the USDOI (BLM) to address a specialized function. The Incident Command System (ICS) does not presently include this position in the organization but uses the term Airtanker Coordinator (ATCO). The differences between the functions of the two positions are addressed below.

Leadplane operations place a high demand on not only pilot skills, but on a person's management skills. Pilot skills, mission management, and application of fire behavior knowledge, all correlate with successful mission performance.

a) Definitions

vi) **Airtanker Coordinator (ATCO)** – The Airtanker Coordinator is a position recognized in the ICS. The primary duties of the ATCO are to provide for the safe and efficient operation of airtanker aircraft over an incident. The ATCO is an airborne position and is supervised by the ATGS. The duties of the ATCO may be fulfilled by the ATGS. Some agencies assign the duties of the ATCO and those of the ATGS to one individual. Other agencies assign the duties to either one or two individuals depending on the complexity and geographic location of the incident. The position of ATCO does not require the incumbent to be a pilot. The ATCO is not authorized for low-level flight (flight below 500 feet above ground level).

vii) **Leadplane Pilot** – The Leadplane pilot is a position authorized by some agencies whose primary duties are the same as those of the Airtanker Coordinator. Therefore, the Leadplane pilot is classified as an ATCO in the ICS. While the Leadplane and ATCO positions share the same mission, the operational methods to accomplish the mission differ significantly. The Leadplane is authorized to fly low-level patterns (below 500 feet above ground level) over the incident area to facilitate airtanker drops (Special Use for DOI). The Leadplane pilot position is always filled by a qualified pilot. The primary purpose of the Leadplane is to provide for a safe and efficient aerial application operation in the hazardous low level environment over an incident.

b) **Leadplane Pilot Qualifications, Training, Certification, and Currency**

The primary mission of the Leadplane pilot is to ensure the safe, efficient and effective use of airtankers in the management of wildland fire or other incidents. An interagency Leadplane pilot call sign/qualification list is maintained by the USFS WO and published annually in the *National Mobilization Guide*.

i)   **Qualifications** – Candidates for Leadplane pilot designation must be federal or State (or state contract) employees who have the appropriate FAA pilot and medical certifications. Forest Service candidates shall possess, as a minimum, the flight experience listed in FSH 5709.16. Department of The Interior (DOI) pilots shall meet, as a minimum, the requirements of 351 DM 3. State contract employees shall posses, at a minimum, the flight experience listed in FSH 5709.16 Trainees shall complete the mission training and certification requirements of this section.

(1)   **Deviations or Exceptions** – The National Aviation Operations Officer (USFS), the National Aviation Program Manager (BLM), or CAFFIRE Chief of Aviation may authorize deviations or exceptions from the training requirements. Approved deviations or exceptions will be in writing. The National Leadplane Program Coordinator (USFS) or the National Aviation Management Specialist (BLM) will maintain copies of the approval and a copy will be carried in the trainees Training Folder.

(a)   **Requests for Deviations or Exceptions** – Requests for deviations or exceptions from the required training will be in writing from the RAO (USFS) or NAO (BLM).

(b)   **Justification** – The justification for the request shall be based on a substantial amount of previous aerial firefighting experience.

(2)   **Mentor Program** – Each Leadplane pilot trainee shall be assigned a Mentor by their supervisor. Mentors shall be employees with a minimum of two season's experience as a qualified Leadplane pilot. The program is designed to help bring along new Leadplane pilots into the system and to make these persons a stronger, more rounded aerial firefighter. The mentor will:

(a)   Help develop a training plan for the candidate

(b)   Assure training is on track and that all requirements are being scheduled so as to not delay progress

(c)   Assist with any problems regarding agency and training requirements

ii) **Training** – This defines the Leadplane pilot mission-training syllabus. Prior to initiating training, a Leadplane Check Pilot shall evaluate the trainee's experience. Areas lacking basic skills shall be noted and the candidate recommended for additional training beyond the normal requirements.

(1) **Organizational Training**

   (a) I-200 Basic Incident Command System (ICS)

   (b) S-370 Intermediate Aviation Operations, if available. If not available, S-270 Basic Aviation Operations will suffice

   (c) S-290 Intermediate Fire Behavior

   (d) S-378 Air Tactical Group Supervisor or CALFIRE Air Attack Academy

   (e) Initial Leadplane Pilot Training Course

   Note: The above courses shall be completed **prior to** entering Phase 3 Operational Flight Training.

   (f) Additional courses to be completed within 2 years after initial qualification:

   (i) Crew Resource Management (CRM)

   (ii) National Aerial Firefighting Academy (NAFA) or NAFA flight simulation.

   (g) Candidates will be evaluated on their experience in the following disciplines to determine additional recommended training. Candidates with little or no experience in one or more of these disciplines will obtain additional training and exposure prior to proceeding with Operational Training.

   (i) Wildland fire suppression experience

   (ii) Low level and mountain flying experience

   (iii) Fire suppression tactics

(2) **Operational Ground Training** – The operational elements of the Leadplane mission require both ground and flight instruction during simulated and actual fire missions to meet requirements. The curriculum shall include observing and participating where possible in the following operations

   (a) Helicopter operations

   (b) Ground fire operations on actual fires including actual retardant drops from both airtankers and helitankers

   (c) Airtanker base operations

   (d) Dispatch Center orientation and operations

(3) **Prerequisite Flight Training**

    (a) The Leadplane candidate shall be competent in all FAA defined VFR and IFR flight requirements in high performance, light twin engine airplanes (reference FAA Commercial, Instrument, and Multiengine Practical Test Standards).

    (b) Possess a current agency 12 month VFR and 6 month IFR check (if aircraft is IFR approved).

    (c) The Leadplane candidate shall have completed initial make and model qualifications and have 5 hours PIC in make and model within the last 90 days prior to initiating Operational Flight Training (OFT).

(4) **Operational Flight Training (OFT)** – OFT is divided into three phases. Each phase is to be completed before progressing to the next phase. The sequencing of training within each phase shall be followed as closely as possible. Identified deficiencies shall be corrected and documented before candidate's progress to the next phase.

Note: Phases identify **minimum requirements**. Additional training and missions are often required for a variety of reasons, i.e.: lack of exposure to a mix of situations and complexities, slow progress due to irregularity in training opportunities, low fire experience, lack of multi-region experience etc.

    (a) **Flight Training Records** – Leadplane Pilot Instructors (LPI) will provide the trainee with a written evaluation of each training flight using the three-part Leadplane Training / Check Form. The original copy will be retained by the trainee in their training folder. A copy of the phase completion form will be sent to the National Leadplane Program Coordinator (USFS), the National Aviation Management Specialist (BLM), or agency program manager. The LPI will retain a copy for their records.

    (b) **Leadplane Training / Check Form** – The Leadplane / Check Form is to be used to record all Leadplane training and checkrides. Any above Average (+), Below Average (-), or Unsatisfactory (U) ratings require an explanation in the remarks portion of the form.

    (c) **Annual Review** – Trainees will be reviewed annually by the Leadplane Check Pilot Cadre to monitor progress. A summary of the review will go to the Regional Aviation Officer / National Aviation Management Specialist and the trainees Mentor.

(d) **Initial Training** – Every effort shall be made to limit the number of Leadplane Pilot Instructors assigned to provide training for each candidate during Phases 1 and 2.

(e) **Initial Leadplane Pilot Training Course** – The Initial Leadplane Pilot Training Course should be taken before entering Phase 1 but shall be accomplished before completing Phase 2.

    (i) **Phase 1**

        1. **Minimum** of 10 hours flying, assisting in flight, or observing in flight, actual ATGS fire missions.

        2. **Minimum** of 5 hours of Leadplane Tactical Flight Training comprised of low level flight, mountainous terrain flight, proximity flight, and Leadplane/airtanker simulation. Note: Flight time obtained in the Initial Leadplane Pilot Training Course can be used to meet this requirement.

        3. **Phase Check** – A flight check will be conducted by an LPI. This check will thoroughly evaluate the following in a non-fire environment.

            a. **Oral** – The trainee shall pass an oral review covering all activities under Phase 1. The oral will consist of questions involving (1) specific safety-of-flight and key operational issues, (2) discussion questions designed to determine if the trainee has the base knowledge that should be gained from Phase 1 activities, and (3) general questions to establish that the trainee has an understanding of the operational issues that are necessary to progress to Phase 2 (Appendix B).

            b. **Flight Check:** The flight check shall include low-level mountain flying, airspeed control, tactical low level patterns and join ups.

    (ii) **Phase 2**

        1. **Minimum** of 10 hours as an observer in the right seat on actual fire missions with a LPI.

        2. Flights as observer in a mix of airtankers.

        3. **Minimum** of 15 Leadplane missions on actual fires of various size and complexity as the flying pilot in the left seat under the supervision of a LPI.

Note: The LPI will regularly alternate between the left and right (front and back) seats during Phases 2 and 3 in order to maintain Leadplane pilot proficiency and reinforce techniques and standards.

Note: It is important that the trainee receive timely feedback from airtanker pilots in Phases 2 and 3. When possible, operate from the Airtanker Base or recover back to the base after a mission. This allows for pre and post mission briefings with airtanker crews and airtanker base personnel.

4. **Phase Check** – A Leadplane Check Pilot will administer the Phase Check.

   a. **Oral** – The trainee shall pass an oral review covering all activities under Phase 2. The oral will consist of questions involving (1) specific safety-of-flight and key operational issues, (2) discussion questions designed to determine if the trainee has the base knowledge that should be gained from Phase 2 activities, and (3) questions designed to determine that the trainee has the knowledge to address situations that can arise when performing the Leadplane mission.

   b. **Flight Check** – The flight check to determine that the trainee (1) can safely perform the Leadplane mission, (2) operate within the designated mission profiles, and (3) determine if the trainee has been exposed to varying fire size and complexities. Any identified problem areas will be satisfactorily resolved.

   c. If a trainee does not receive a recommendation for the Phase 2 flight review after completing 25 left seat Phase 2 missions, a progress review may be given by the Agency Leadplane Program Coordinator, or designated Check Pilot. An evaluation flight may be given if deemed necessary by the Leadplane Cadre Steering Chairperson.

(iii) **Phase 3** – All required ground training shall be completed prior to initiating Phase 3.

1. **Minimum** of 10 Leadplane missions on actual fires of varying size and complexities as the flying pilot under the supervision of a LPI.

2. A portion of the Leadplane missions shall be flown in other Regions/States if not accomplished in Phase 2.

3. Additional flights in airtankers

4. **Final Leadplane Progress Check:** A Leadplane Instructor Pilot will make a final progress check upon completion of the Phase 3 Leadplane pilot missions. This will consist of an oral review covering all aspects of Leadplane pilot operations.

5. **Complete Records Review:** Complete records review of the training folder by the candidate's mentor to determine that all requirements have been met and signed off and a review to assure any noted deficiencies have been corrected and the correction documented. The mentor will present the completed package to the Regional Aviation Officer (RAO) / BLM National Aviation Office (NAO) for endorsement. Once received, the mentor will then schedule the final evaluation with a USFS Washington Office, BLM NAO, an out-of-region Leadplane Check Pilot, or agency program manager.

iii) **Certification**

(1) **Documentation of Training** – The pilot is responsible for maintaining their individual training folder. The folder shall include the following:

(a) Course completion certificates.

(b) Record of ground and flight training including documentation of corrected deficiencies.

(c) Sign-offs for each Phase of OFT.

(d) Endorsement from the RAO, BLM NAO, or agency program manager.

(2) **Final Evaluation and Qualification** – To be designated as a Leadplane pilot, candidates shall have:

(a) Satisfactorily completed all organizational and operational flight training and acquired the necessary operational flight experience.

(b) Undergone a complete oral and operational evaluation. The evaluation consists of:

> (i) A Phase 3 sign-off by a LPI who has instructed the candidate during Phase 3, attesting to the candidate's mission competence.

> (ii) A final flight check (which may require multiple missions to allow the Check Pilot to observe adequate performance in complex environments) by a an (or other agency) Leadplane Check Pilot certifying that the candidate has completed the required training and recommends they be approved to perform the Leadplane pilot mission.

> (iii) A Leadplane pilot designation letter from the USFS National Aviation Operations Officer-Operations (NAOO-O)/ National Fixed Wing Standardization Officer (NFWSO)/BLM NAO, or agency program manager approving the designation. A copy shall be forwarded to the appropriate State or National Program Manager.

(3) **Post Qualification Progress Evaluation** – At least one evaluation shall be performed by a designated Leadplane Check Pilot to verify the newly designated Leadplane pilot is performing satisfactorily. This evaluation shall be coordinated by the USFS WO/BLM NAO and conducted during the first year after initial qualification. The evaluation will be performed on a no-notice basis. The results will be forwarded to the RAO/BLM NAO and the Leadplane pilot briefed on the evaluation.

(4) **Air Tactical Pilot/ASM Training** – Following full Leadplane qualification, Leadplane Pilots are required to acquire one year of proven Leadplane experience in multiple geographic regions prior to attending ATP/ASM training.

(5) **MAFFS Qualification** – MAFFS qualification is an additional required endorsement. Leadplane pilots are required to attend the first available MAFFS training session after initial Leadplane qualification.

(6) **VLAT Qualification** – VLAT qualification is an additional required endorsement. Leadplane Pilots are required to complete VLAT training at the earliest opportunity following MAFFS qualification.

(7) **Southern California Qualification** - Leadplane pilots shall receive instruction by an experienced LPI or designee during a fire mission, or series of missions as appropriate, in Southern California and Los Angeles County before operating alone in that area. The Leadplane Cadre Chairperson may waive this requirement if the Leadplane

Pilot received instruction in this area on actual fire missions during Phase II or Phase III Leadplane training.

iv) **Leadplane Pilot Currency**

(1) **Recent Experience** – Leadplane pilots shall complete 30 Leadplane missions in a three-year period. Pilots not meeting the 30-mission requirement shall pass a flight check on an actual Leadplane fire mission with a Leadplane Check Pilot.

Leadplane Mission – A mission consists of a flight on an actual fire where retardant is dropped. Each additional fire flown during a single flight counts as an additional mission.

(2) **Currency Training** – Leadplane pilots shall receive the following currency training:

(a) **Annually Receive Recurrent Flight and Ground Training**

(i) Ground training shall include

1. Target Description Exercise

2. Safety Review (Pertinent Incident/Accidents, Standard Fire Orders/Watch-Out Conditions)

3. Communications

4. Tactics

5. Incident Command System

6. Pre-season Update: (Airtanker crew assignments, Expected fire behavior, Long-term weather prognosis)

(ii) Flight Training shall be a minimum of 3 flight hours and include:

1. Training

   a. Fire size-up

   b. Target Description

   c. Leadplane Tactical Flight Training

   d. Communications

   e. Escape Routes

   f. Emergency Procedures

2. Annual Leadplane pilot mission competency check by a Leadplane Check Pilot

(3) **Standardization Evaluation** – Random Leadplane mission checks will be conducted for all qualified Leadplane pilots. A Leadplane check pilot will perform the evaluation on a no-notice basis. The

results will be forwarded to the RAO/BLM NAO and the Leadplane pilot briefed on the evaluation.

(4) **Supplemental (AD) Leadplane Pilots** – AD pilots shall maintain the same currency and training requirements stipulated for agency pilots. The USFS WO will publish a list of supplemental Leadplane pilots on an annual basis.

c) **Modular Airborne Fire Fighting System (MAFFS)**

i) Qualifications

(1) Be a qualified Leadplane pilot

(2) Shall have completed MAFFS Leadplane Pilot training

(3) Shall have acquired significant Leadplane experience as determined by the USDA-FS National MAFFS Program Manager

ii) Training – Attend the MAFFS Training Session each fourth year.

iii) Certification

(1) Complete the MAFFS Training Session and pass a check flight administered by a Leadplane Check Pilot.

(2) Interim certification may be granted upon initial Leadplane qualification based on actual MAFFS operational experience obtained during initial Leadplane training. The National MAFFS Program Manager shall give this certification. Leadplane pilots who obtain interim MAFFS certification shall attend the next MAFFS Training Session.

iv) Currency – Leadplane pilots shall attend the MAFFS Training Session every four years at a minimum.

d) **Very Large Airtanker (VLAT)**

i) **Qualifications**

(1) Qualified Leadplane Pilot

(2) MAFFS Leadplane Pilot training

(3) VLAT training

ii) **Training**

(1) Review VLAT training presentation (.ppt)

(2) Observe one drop from VLAT flight station

(3) Observe one VLAT operational lead. This can be accomplished during the VLAT ride.

Download the VLAT .ppt from the BLM NIFC Fire and Aviation site at http://www.blm.gov/nifc/st/en/prog/fire/Aviation/aerial_supervision.html

iii) **Certification**

    (1)   Complete VLAT Training.

    (2)   Pass VLAT check flight administered by a VLAT qualified Check Pilot.

iv) **Currency**- Annually review VLAT training presentation (.ppt)

e) **Leadplane Pilot Instructor (LPI)**

  i)   Qualifications

    (1)   Current Leadplane pilot with a minimum of two seasons experience after initial qualification.

    (2)   Multi-Region experience as a qualified Leadplane Pilot.

    (3)   MAFFS (at earliest opportunity)

    (4)   VLAT (at earliest opportunity)

    (5)   Southern California (at earliest opportunity)

  ii) **Nomination Process** – The USFS Leadplane National Standardization Instructor Pilot or BLM National Leadplane Program Manager, in conjunction with the Leadplane Check Pilot Cadre and with concurrence of the appropriate RAO/BLM NAO, or agency program manager will nominate pilots who meet the qualifications and whom they consider to have the experience, aptitude, dedication, and ability to perform the duties of a Leadplane Pilot Instructor (LPI).

  iii) Certification – Pass a Leadplane Pilot Instructor oral and flight check administered by a Leadplane Check Pilot.

  iv) A Leadplane pilot instructor designation letter from the USFS NAOO-O/ NFWSO/BLM NAO, or agency program manager approving the designation. A copy shall be forwarded to the appropriate State or National Program Manager.

  v) Training (Reserved)

  vi) Currency – An LPI shall:

    (1)   Maintain Leadplane pilot currency

    (2)   Maintain MAFFS and VLAT currency requirements

    (3)   Pass an LPI oral and flight check administered by a Leadplane Check Pilot (biennially).

f) **Leadplane Check Pilot**

  i)   Qualifications

    (1)   A minimum of five seasons of operational Leadplane experience

    (2)   A minimum of three seasons as an active LPI

(3) Possess the appropriate FAA Flight Instructor Certificates

ii) **Nomination Process** – The USFS Leadplane National Standardization Pilot or BLM National Leadplane Program Manager, in conjunction with the Leadplane Check Pilot Cadre and with concurrence of the appropriate RAO/BLM NAO, will nominate pilots who meet the qualifications and have the ability to train and evaluate Leadplane pilots in accordance with the provisions of the IASG.

iii) Certification – Pass a Leadplane Pilot Instructor oral and flight check administered by a Leadplane Check Pilot.

iv) A Leadplane Check Pilot designation letter from the USFS NAOO-O/ NFWSO/BLM NAO, or agency program manager approving the designation. A copy shall be forwarded to the appropriate State or National Program Manager.

v) Training – Attend the biennial Leadplane Check Pilot Cadre Meeting.

(1) Currency – The Leadplane Check Pilot shall

(a) Maintain Leadplane pilot currency requirements

(b) Maintain MAFFS and VLAT currency requirements

(c) Maintain LPI training requirements

(d) Attend the Leadplane Check Pilot Cadre meeting (biennially)

g) **Leadplane Pilot Quality Assurance**

i) **Leadplane Cadre Review Board** – A Leadplane Cadre Review Board may convene when written documentation has been provided to the National Leadplane Program Coordinator identifying nonstandard or deficient mission performance of a qualified Leadplane pilot. The Cadre Review Board shall consist of Leadplane Cadre members (minimum of 3) and will be assembled for the purpose of ensuring quality and standardization among the Leadplane pilot community.

ii) **Review Board Process** – Upon assembly, the review board will ascertain the validity and severity of the matter in question, after which it will establish the necessary course of action. Optional responses in the event of a potential review may include:

(1) Dismiss the claim if unable to verify or substantiate performance deficiencies.

(2) Recommend appropriate training specific to any identified deficiency.

(3) Appoint an out of region check pilot to perform a check flight(s). The check flight may be performed in a training or fire environment as directed by the Cadre Review Board.

      (4)   Recommend suspension of the Leadplane pilot's qualifications pending further investigation.

    iii)   **Review Board Findings and Documentation** – Upon completion of the review process and/or completion of additional required training or check flight(s), the Cadre Review Board will issue a recommendation based on its findings. All documentation, including training records, flight check forms, and review board findings and recommendations shall be forwarded to the individual's supervisor, Regional Aviation Officer/Aviation Manager, the USFS NAOO, or agency program manager. Potential recommendations include:

      (1)   Return pilot to full operational status.

      (2)   Initiate further training and/or check flights.

      (3)   Revoke Leadplane qualification.

3) Aerial Supervision Module (ASM)

a) Introduction

An ASM is a crew of two specially trained individuals who retain their individual Leadplane Pilot and ATGS qualifications. Each crewmember has specific duties and responsibilities that fall within their area of expertise. These vary in scope based on the mission and task loads of each crewmember. The Air Tactical Pilot (ATP) serves as the aircraft commander and is primarily responsible for aircraft coordination over the incident.

The Air Tactical Supervisor (ATS) serves as the mission commander who develops/implements strategy/tactics in conjunction with the Incident Commander (IC) and operations personnel. When no IC is present the ATS assumes those responsibilities until qualified ground personnel arrive.

The ASM is designed for initial attack operations, but can provide incident management teams with the flexibility of being able to alternate between operational functions until dedicated aerial supervision resources can be assigned to the incident.

b) ASM Positions

    iv)   **Air Tactical Pilot (ATP)** – The ATP is the aircraft commander and works in a team concept with the ATS by soliciting input and sharing information regarding aerial fire suppression assets, operations, performance, and safety using crew resource management (CRM) skills. Responsibilities are consistent with the traditional role of the Leadplane pilot.

    v)   **Air Tactical Supervisor (ATS)** – The ATS is the mission commander and works as a team member with the ATP by soliciting input and sharing information regarding aerial fire suppression assets, operations, performance, and safety using CRM skills. Responsibilities are consistent with the traditional role of the ATGS.

c) **ASM Resource Status, Ordering, and Identification**

ASM resource identification and status are reported using the following procedures:

i) **Tactical Aircraft Report** – The National Interagency Coordination Center (NICC) and Geographic Area Coordination Centers (GACC) report the status of the ASM crews as a national resource. The ATPs Leadplane Pilot designator is used in conjunction the federal ASM designator B (Bravo) to identify the ASM. For example, when Lead 03 is teamed with an ATS, they become Bravo-3. The State of Alaska ASM designator is A, Alpha. The CALFIRE ASM designator is C, Charlie.

ii) **Resource Ordering** – Federal Aerial Supervision Modules are a national resource and will be ordered in the same manner as Leadplanes or other national resources. Individual crewmembers (ATS or ATP) are ordered as a name request through ROSS as ATGS or Leadplane pilot.

d) **Base of Operation**

The ASM is flexible and can be operated from any Air Attack/Fixed-Wing Base, but it is recommended that the ASM base of operations be at an airtanker base. This allows for pre- and post-briefings with the airtanker crews and base personnel. (See National & GACC Mob Guides.)

e) **Flight and Duty Day Limitations**

The ATS attached to an ASM will have the same flight and duty limitation as the ATP. Flight or duty limitations may be exceeded at the discretion of the ATS during high fire activity if aerial supervision resources are limited and there are threats to public and firefighter safety. Such occurrences must be documented and forwarded to the Agency Program Manager.

f) **Crew Utilization other than ASM Configuration**

The ASM is a shared national Resource. Any operations that would limit the status of this resource, including single pilot lead operations, need to be approved by the Agency Program Manager, in concurrence with the flight crew.

g) **Authorized Passengers**

The following positions are authorized to be on board the aircraft during ASM operations:

i) Air Tactical Pilot/Air Tactical Pilot Trainee

ii) Instructor Pilot/Check Pilot

iii) Air Tactical Supervisor/Air Tactical Supervisor Trainee

iv)   Instructor ATS/Check ATS

v)   Leadplane Pilot Trainee

vi)   Other personnel must be authorized in writing by the Agency Program Manager and approved by the flight crew. This is generally limited to three total personnel on board the aircraft during low-level fire operations

h)   ASM Training and Checks

Crews that are scheduled to be working together as primaries will attend ASM/CRM training as a team. Completion of ASM/CRM training is required of both crewmembers prior to low-level (ASM) operations. If both individuals have worked a season as primary ASM crewmembers and previously attended the training, they are exempt from this requirement.

i)   ATP Training and Check Ride

    (1)   Initial Leadplane Pilot Training: Prior to qualification as ATP each pilot will be trained as a standalone Leadplane pilot.

    (2)   ASM/ATP check: Leadplane pilots transitioning into the Aerial Supervision Module are required to pass a check-ride administered by either a Check-ATP or Check-ATS. For Leadplane pilots entering the program within one year of LP qualification, this checkride is required to take place on an active fire. All other checks can be done during simulated exercises.

ii)   ATP Currency – ATP will complete 5 missions/year. These missions can be considered Leadplane missions for the purpose of maintaining Leadplane currency. Single role Leadplane missions do not count towards ATP currency. ATPs not meeting the 5 mission requirement will be required to pass a mission check ride on an actual or simulated mission conducted by a check pilot or check ATS.

i)   Initial Air Tactical Supervisor Training

i)   Objective: To establish the qualification and training requirements necessary to perform as an Air Tactical Supervisor (ATS) attached to an Aerial Supervision Module (ASM) that performs low-level flight operations.

ii)   ATS candidates will be referred to the ASM cadre by the ATGS Cadre after becoming an ATGS Instructor. Candidates will have demonstrated superior ATGS skills during high complexity fire situations in various geographic areas and fuel types. CALFIRE requires 3 seasons of assigned experience following the initial ATGS qualification.

iii) Documentation of Training – It is the responsibility of the ATS candidate to maintain and update a training and experience folder which will include

    (1) Course completion certificates

    (2) Completed ATGS task book, or copy of Red Card Qualification

    (3) Documentation of initial flight check issued by a Check ATS

    (4) Annual update of experience to agency specific Incident Qualification and Certification System

    (5) Documentation of annual ASM in-flight recurrent training Letter of Authorization signed by the agency ASM Program Manager

    (6) The Agency Program Manager maintains copies of the ATS Letter of Authorization and documentation of annual recurrent training

iv) Initial ATS Training and Evaluation – An assigned ASM mentor/ATS instructor will oversee the candidate's training and tailor the candidate's curriculum based upon previous training and experience. The minimum fireline qualification for an ATS trainee is ATGS. Upon successful completion of all ATS task and course requirements, an ATS Instructor forwards the recommendation for certification to a Check ATS. The Check ATS reviews the candidate's training documentation, experience, and conducts a flight check on an actual incident to determine that the trainee can safely perform the ASM mission. When the candidate is approved, the Check ATS forwards the nominee's authorization and endorsement to the Agency Program Manager, who issues a Letter of Authorization to the supervisor.

    (1) Air Tactical Supervisor Training Syllabus

        (a) Initial Training Requirements

            (i) Nationally approved CRM Training – prior to full qualification

            (ii) Initial ASM/CRM Training

            (iii) ATS Task Book Completion

            (iv) Observation flights: Two observation flights must be completed prior to front seat flight training. One of these flights must occur on an actual fire mission.

            (v) Flight Training: An ATS (I) will be on board the aircraft for all training missions. The ATS (I) will determine when the trainee is authorized to continue training with the ATP (I) or (C).

            (vi) ATS Flight Check: The flight check should be administered by an individual other that the primary instructor.

v) The following table identifies all possible ASM crew configurations and the authorizations of each ASM position.

Table 1. ASM Training and Flight Authorization

Personnel listed in the first column are authorized to fly with, instruct, check, observe, or are not authorized to fly with the personnel listed across the top row.

Key - F: Fly in front crew position; **I:** Instruct; **C:** Check; **O:** Observe; **T:** Trainee; **NA:** Not Authorized.

	ATS	ATS (I)	ATS (C)	ATS (T)	ATP	ATP (I)	ATP (C)	ATP (T)
ATS	F	F	F	NA	F	F	F	NA
ATS (I)	F, I	F, I	F	F, I	F, I	F	F	F, I
ATS (C)	F, I, C	F, I, C	F, I, C	F, I, C	F, I, C	F, I, C	F, I, C	F, I, C
ATS (T)	O	O, F	O, F	NA	O	O, F	O, F	NA
ATP	F	F	F	NA	O, F	O, F	O, F	NA
ATP (I)	F, I	F, I	F	F, I	F, I	F, I	F	F, I
ATP (C)	F, I, C	F, I, C	F, I, C	F, I, C	F, I, C	F, I, C	F, I, C	F, I, C
ATP (T)	O	O, F	O, F	NA	O	O, F	O, F	NA

j) Post ATS Qualification Recommendations & Target Dates

i) Private Pilot Ground School/Private Pilot Rating - First Year

ii) Current Fireline Qualification (Every 5 Years)

iii) **Recommendations** – Fireline assignments with local initial attack resources should be secured to maintain perspective and enhance credibility with operations personnel. ATS fireline qualifications that should be maintained include, but are not limited to:

(1) Incident Commander - Type 3

(2) Division Group Supervisor

(3) Strike Team / Task Force Leader

k) ATS Currency Requirements

An ATS must complete and document five ASM missions per year and attend an ASM refresher every 3 years. The annual mission summary will be forwarded to the Agency Program Manager. Failure to maintain these qualifications results in a lapse in currency and requires a check ride on an actual/simulated airborne fire mission utilizing aerial resources by a qualified Check ATS or ATP Check Pilot. If currency lapses for 3 or more years, the check ride must be performed on an actual mission.

l) ATS Currency Training

Currency training provides qualified ATS's with aircraft familiarization, ASM Crew Resource Management (CRM) training, and mission refresher exercises. ASM/CRM refresher training includes: discussion of the concepts and practices of CRM, teamwork, effective communication practices, aircraft familiarization, and at least one simulation flight.

m) ATS Instructor Requirements

  i) Qualifications

    (1) Current ATS with a minimum of two consecutive seasons' experience after initial qualification or primary ATS attached to an ASM with one full season's experience

    (2) Multi-regional experience

    (3) Pass an initial flight check administered by a check ATS

  ii) Nomination Process – ASM program personnel nominate individuals who meet the qualifications and who they consider to have the experience, aptitude, dedication, and ability to perform the duties as an ATS instructor. The ATS Cadre reviews the qualifications and experience of each nominee before recommending their selection to the Agency Program Manager, who adds this designation to the Letter of Authorization.

  iii) ATS Instructor Currency

    (1) Maintain ATS currency.

    (2) Annually document 5 ATS instructor missions or Biennially pass an ATS flight check administered by a Check ATS

n) Check ATS and ASM Cadre Requirements

  i) Qualifications

    (1) Three consecutive years as a fully qualified ATS

    (2) 1 full season as an ATS Instructor with diverse experience in different regions

    (3) Current ATS Instructor

  ii) Nomination Process: ASM Program Managers, in conjunction with the ATS Cadre, nominate ATS Instructors who meet the requirements and have demonstrated the ability to instruct and evaluate ATS's in the mission environment. Upon their endorsement of the nominee, the ATS Cadre forwards the recommendation to the Agency Program Manager, who adds this designation to the ATS's Letter of Authorization.

  iii) Check ATS Currency

    (1) Maintain ATS currency.

    (2) Maintain ATS Instructor currency.

    (3) Attend yearly ASM Cadre meeting.

Chapter 4 – Policies, Regulations, and Guidelines

Incident aviation operations are often conducted under adverse flight conditions. Congested airspace, reduced visibility, poor weather and mountainous terrain all add risk and complexity to operations.

Complexity dictates the level of supervision required to safely and effectively conduct aerial operations. Aerial supervision may be provided by a Leadplane, ATCO, ASM, ATGS or HLCO. Dispatchers and Airtanker Base Managers, in consultation with aerial supervisors, are mutually responsible for ensuring that policies are applied and limitations not exceeded.

1) Retardant operations and low light conditions (sunrise/sunset)

Multi-engine airtankers shall be dispatched to arrive over a fire not earlier than 30 minutes after official sunrise and not later than 30 minutes before official sunset. Retardant operations will only be conducted during daylight hours. Retardant operations are permitted after official sunset, but must have concurrence by the involved flight crews. In addition, aerial supervision (Lead, ATCO, ASM, or ATGS) must be on scene. Daylight hours are defined as 30 minutes prior to sunrise until 30 minutes after sunset as noted in the table below. Flights by multi-engine aircraft to assigned bases may occur after daylight hours.

Figure 3. Multi-engine Airtanker Startup and Cutoff Regulations

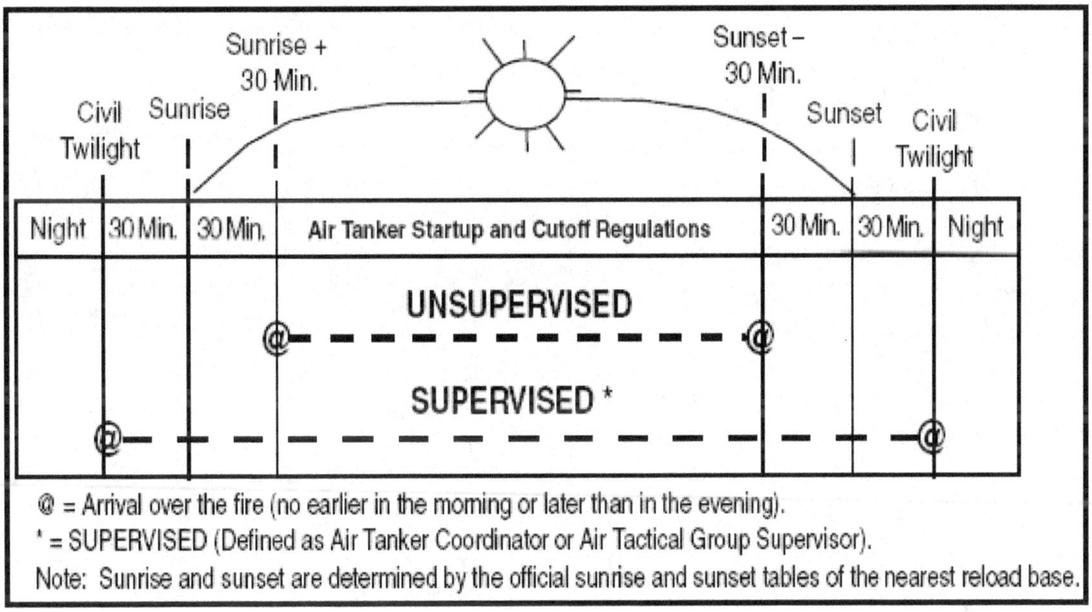

@ = Arrival over the fire (no earlier in the morning or later than in the evening).
* = SUPERVISED (Defined as Air Tanker Coordinator or Air Tactical Group Supervisor).
Note: Sunrise and sunset are determined by the official sunrise and sunset tables of the nearest reload base.

    a) In Alaska an airtanker pilot shall not be authorized to drop retardant during periods outside of civil twilight (see glossary).

    b) Single engine airtankers (SEATs) and helicopters are limited to flight during the official daylight hours.

c) Flight crews might experience late dawn or early dusk conditions based on terrain features and sun angle, and flight periods should be adjusted accordingly. Daylight hours may be further limited at the discretion of the pilot, aviation manager, ATGS, ASM, or Leadplane because of low visibility conditions caused by smoke, shadows or other environmental factors.

d) **Aerial Supervision Requirements**

Table 2. Incident Aerial Supervision Requirements

When aerial supervision resources are co-located with retardant aircraft, they should be launched together on the initial order to maximize safety, effectiveness, and efficiency of incident operations. Incidents with 3 or more aircraft over/assigned to them should have aerial supervision over/assigned the incident. Federal policy dictates additional requirements as listed below.

Situation	Lead/ATCO/ASM	ATGS
Airtanker not IA rated.	Required if no ATGS	Required if no Lead/ATCO/ASM
MAFFS	MAFFS Qualified LEAD/ASM	*****
VLAT	VLAT Qualified Lead/ASM	*****
When requested by airtanker, ATGS, Lead, ATCO, or ASM	Required	Required
Foreign Government airtankers.	Required if no ATGS	Required if no Lead/ATCO/ASM
Multi-engine airtanker: Retardant drops conducted between 30 minutes prior to, and 30 minutes after sunrise, or 30 minutes prior to sunset to 30 minutes after sunset.	Required if no ATGS	Required if no Lead/ATCO/ASM
Single engine airtanker (SEAT): SEATS are required to be "on the ground" by ½ hour after sunset.	See level 2 SEAT requirements	See level 2 SEAT requirements
Level 2 SEAT requirements: Level 2 rated SEAT operating over an incident with more than one other tactical aircraft on scene.	Required if no ATGS	Required if no Lead/ATCO/ASM
Retardant drops in congested/urban interface areas.	Order	May use if no Lead/ATCO/ASM
Periods of marginal weather, poor visibility or turbulence.	Order	Order

2) Definitions of key aerial supervision terms

a) **Required**: Aerial supervisory resource(s) that shall be over the incident when specified air tactical operations are being conducted.

b) **Ordered**: Aerial supervisory resources that shall be ordered by the controlling entity (Air tactical operations may be continued while the aerial supervision resource is enroute to the incident. Operations can be continued if the resource is not available.)

c) **Over**: The air tactical resource is flying above or is in a holding pattern adjacent to the incident.

d) **Assigned**: Tactical resource allocated to an incident. The resource may be flying enroute to and from, or on hold at a ground site.

3) Instances when aerial airtanker supervision is not required

a) **Multiengine Airtankers** – Except for conditions identified in the aerial supervision requirements table, an airtanker crewed by an initial attack rated captain may be dispatched to drop on a fire without aerial supervision.

b) **Single Engine Airtankers (SEATs)** – Don't require supervision except as noted previously in this section.

4) SEAT policy

Under the Incident Command System airtankers carrying 799 gallons or less, are classified as Type 4 airtankers (SEATs). SEATs are generally used for initial attack and aerial supervision is usually not required. Type 4 airtankers are generally used for initial attack; typically for distances up to 75 nautical miles from their reload base. Therefore, aerial supervision may not be necessary or required. When a Leadplane, ATCO, ASM or ATGS is providing aerial supervision over an incident using Type 4 airtankers, the operational limitations of this chapter apply in addition to the following:

All SEATs, including Type 3 approved Air Tractor AT-802's, are subject to the same operational limitations.

There are an increasing number of SEATs that have a capacity of up to 799 gallons. There are some Air Tractor, AT-802's that fully meet the Airtanker Boards tank and door requirements to be classified as Type 3 Airtankers. Of these, only a few have acquired the Airtanker Board's approval. These are contracted for 800 gallons. Those that either do not meet the tank or door requirements (constant flow system), or meet them and have not sought Airtanker Board approval, are contracted for 799 gallons. All SEATs, except the 800 gallon AT-802's certified by the Airtanker Board, are issued 400 series airtanker numbers. The SEATs classified as type 3 are assigned an 800 series identifier.

a) **Radios** – Two panel-mounted VHF-AM (VHF-1, VHF-2) aeronautical transceivers, each with a minimum of 760 channels.

b) **Landing Sites** – Use of off-airport landing sites must be authorized by agency policy. SEATs pilots will approve all landing sites for safety and suitability.

c) **Landing Loaded** – Unless dictated by an emergency, SEATs are not to land loaded.

d) **Wind Limits** – 30 kts sustained or 15 kt gust spread

See the *Interagency SEAT Operations Guide* for further guidance

5) Foreign Government Aircraft on United States Incidents

Under international cooperative agreements the USDA-FS, USDI-BLM and state agencies may enlist the assistance of Canadian air tactical resources on United States' incidents. A Canadian Air Attack Officer flying in a Bird Dog or Leadplane aircraft will normally come with Canadian airtankers. The Canadian Airtanker communications system is compatible with USDA-FS and USDI Systems. Aerial supervisors assigned to these incidents will adhere to the following policies and guidelines:

a) **Incidents on Federal Lands**

    i)   Aerial Supervision shall be assigned to the incident as outlined in the *Incident Aerial Supervision Requirements* table in this chapter.

    ii)   A U.S. federal ATGS, ASM, or Leadplanes shall supervise Canadian airtankers. In the absence of a Leadplane or ASM, the Canadian Air Attack Officer/Bird Dog is authorized to direct Canadian airtanker drops. **Deviations from this policy must be specifically approved by the appropriate agency.**

    iii)   Airtanker Reloads – The reload base for Canadian airtankers shall be determined by the originating dispatch.

    iv)   Canadian airtanker pilots shall be briefed on standard drop height minimums as they normally drop from lower heights.

    v)   Canadian airtankers and helicopters operating on Federal lands will be managed in the same manner as United States resources.

b) **Incidents on Cooperator Lands** – When an ATGS, ASM or Lead are assigned to a cooperator incident employing Canadian air resources; the incident will be managed as outlined in above in this chapter.

c) **Authorization to Lead United States Airtankers** – Only federally (U.S.A.) approved Leadplane/ASM pilots are authorized to lead United States federally procured airtankers on airtanker drops. Canadian Air Attack Officers/Bird Dogs are not authorized to "lead" U.S. tankers.

6) Flight Condition Guidelines

Aerial Supervision personnel must carefully evaluate flight hazards, conditions (visibility, wind, thunder cells, turbulence, and terrain) to ensure that operations can be conducted in a safe and effective manner. The following policies and guidelines are designed to do this:

a) **Visibility**

Regardless of time of day, when poor visibility precludes safe operations, flights will be suspended. It is recommended that incident aircraft fly with landing and strobe lights on at all times. It is required that Leadplanes fly with landing/impulse and strobe lights on at all times. Regular position reporting is critical in marginal visibility conditions.

b) Wind Conditions

Moderate to high winds and turbulent conditions affect flight safety and water/retardant drop effectiveness. The following guidelines should be considered in making the decision to continue or suspend operations. A number of factors including terrain, fuel type, target location, resources at risk, cross- winds, etc., must be considered.

i)   **Heavy Airtanker Drops** – Generally ineffective in winds over 20-25 kts.

ii) **SEAT Operations** – Generally ineffective in wind over 15-20 kts. Operations shall be suspended when sustained winds are 30 kts or the gust spread is 15 kts.

iii) **Helitanker Drops** – Generally ineffective in winds over 25-30 kts.

iv) **Helicopter Operations** – Capability to fly in excessive wind conditions varies considerably with weight class (type) of the helicopter and degree of turbulence. If the helicopter flight manual or the helicopter operators policy does not set lower limits, the following shall be used, but may be further restricted at the pilot's or air operations personnel's discretion. Limits are as follows:

(1) Above 500' AGL: All helicopter types: constant winds up to 50 kts.

(2) Below 500' AGL

(a) **Type 3 Helicopters** – Steady winds shall not exceed 30 kts or a maximum gust spread of 15 knots.

(b) **Type 2 and 1 Helicopters** – Steady winds shall not exceed 40 kts or a maximum gust spread of 15 kts.

c) Thunder Storm

Evaluate "thunder storm activity" and flight safety. Consider delaying operations or reassigning resources to safe operation areas. Suspend flight operations when lightning or other adverse weather conditions are present.

7) Air Attack Pilot Policy

Pilots flying air tactical missions must be Agency approved. Pilot cards must be checked prior to air tactical missions.

a) Air Attack Pilot Approval

Aerial supervision pilots (for ATGS or HLCO) shall be inspected and approved annually by a qualified Forest Service or OAS Pilot Inspector.

Qualification for air tactical missions shall be indicated on the back side of the Airplane Pilot Qualification Card. Pilots being considered for air tactical missions should be experienced aerial observer pilots or pilots with tactical CALFIRE experience.

Note: Helicopter pilots are normally not approved specifically for ATGS or HLCO missions. Pilots who have not flown air tactical missions must be thoroughly briefed before use on air tactical missions.

b) **Pilot Orientation and Training**

Prior to flying their initial air tactical mission, preferably pre-season, the pilot shall receive a basic orientation/training from a qualified ATGS. As a minimum, the following shall be covered:

i) General scope of the mission

ii) Incident air organization – emphasis on ATGS, ASM and HLCO roles

iii) Specific responsibilities of the ATGS

iv) Specific responsibilities and expectations of the ATGS pilot

v) Air resources commonly assigned to, or present on, the type of incident

vi) Communications hardware, procedures, protocol and frequency management

vii) Air space management (TFRs, flight patterns, etc.)

viii) Operations safety

ix) Standard operating procedures

x) Fuel management

xi) Dispatch readiness, availability for duty

xii) Records

8) Personal Protective Equipment (PPE) Policy

a) **The following PPE is required for all interagency ATGS operations: (ATGS and Pilot)**

i) Leather shoes or boots

ii) Full length cotton or Nomex pants or a flight suit.

b) **Leadplane and ASM**

i) **Policy**: The use of PPE by personnel engaged in Leadplane/ASM operations is required as per agency policy. This requirement is stated in various publications, including the USDA Safety and Health Handbook, FSH 6709.11, Chapter 3, the USDI Safety and Health Handbook, 485 DM, Chapter 20, and both departments Aircraft Accident Prevention Plans. Specific requirements for PPE differ slightly among organizations. A complete text of requirements can be found in USDI Departmental Manual (351 DM 1).

(1) Requirements

(a) **Flight Suit** – One-piece fire-resistant polyamide or aramid material or equal. The use of wildland firefighter Nomex shirts and trousers (two-piece) is authorized.

(b) **Protective Footgear** – Leather boots shall extend above the ankle. Such boots may not have synthetic insert panels (such as jungle boots) unless the panels are of a polymide or aramide (Nomex) or polybenzimidazole (PBI), Kevlar, or flame-resistant fabric.

(c) **Gloves** – Gloves made of polyamide or aramid material or all leather gloves, without synthetic liners. Leather gloves must cover wrist and allow required finger dexterity.

(d) **Flight Helmets**

(i) Aerial Supervision from helicopters requires a flight helmet.

(ii) Flight helmets are optional for Forest Service Leadplane pilots.

(iii) BLM pilots shall comply with 351 DM 1, ALSE Handbook and applicable BLM Agency exemptions.

(iv) Alaskan ASM operations are conducted in the Pilatus PC-7, which requires the use of a flight helmet.

c) **Airtanker Pilots**

Airtanker pilots will follow the personal protective equipment requirements as outlined in their contract.

9) Oxygen requirements

Flights using call when needed (CWN) vendors must comply with FAA regulations they operate under.

a) **Part 135** – 14 CFR part 135.89: Supplemental oxygen must be available and used by the flight crew at cabin pressure altitudes above 10,000 feet (MSL) for that portion of the flight more than 30 minutes duration. At cabin pressure altitudes above 12,000 feet (MSL) the flight crew must use supplemental oxygen during the entire flight.

b) **Part 91.211** – Supplemental oxygen must be available and used by the flight crew at cabin pressure altitudes above 12,500 feet (MSL) for that portion of the flight more than 30 minutes duration. At cabin pressure altitudes above 14,000 feet (MSL) the flight crew must use supplemental oxygen during the entire flight. At cabin pressure altitudes above 15,000 feet, (MSL) all passengers must have supplemental oxygen available during the entire flight.

10) Start-up/Cut-off, Flight Time, and Limitations Policy

a) Aircraft

i) **Twin Engine Fixed Wing** – These aircraft are not limited to daylight operations. The aircraft can travel to or work over the incident before sunrise and after sunset as long as the aircraft and pilot are equipped/authorized for IFR operations. Consult agency policy for further clarification.

ii) **Single Engine Fixed Wing** – Flight time is limited to 30 minutes prior to sunrise and 30 minutes after sunset.

iii) **Helicopters** – Flight time is limited to 30 minutes prior to sunrise and 30 minutes after sunset. Multi engine helicopters are not limited to daylight operations under certain stipulations such as emergencies or lighted airports. The IHOG contains the complete policy.

11) Flight Crew Duty Day and Flight Hour Policy

a) Phase 1 – Standard Flight and Duty Limitations

- Fourteen (14) hour maximum duty day.
- Eight (8) hours maximum daily flight time for mission flights.
- Ten (10) hours for point-to-point, with a two (2) pilot crew.
- Maximum cumulative flight hours of thirty-six (36) hours, up to forty-two (42) hours in six (6) days.
- Minimum of ten (10) hours uninterrupted time off (rest) between duty periods.

This does not diminish the authority or obligation of any individual COR (Contracting Officer Representative) or Aviation Manager to impose shorter duty days or additional days off at any time for any flight crew members for fatigue at their discretion, as is currently provided for in agency direction and contract specifications.

b) Interim Flight and Duty Limitations Implementation

During extended periods of a high level of flight activity or maximum 14-hour days, fatigue factors must be taken into consideration by Fire and Aviation Managers. Phase 2 and/or Phase 3 Duty Limitations will be implemented for specific Geographic Area's Aviation resources. The minimum scope of operation should be by Geographic Area, i.e., Northwest, Great Basin, etc.

Implementation decisions will be made on a coordinated, interagency basis, involving the GACC, NICC, NMAC and National Aviation Representatives at NIFC.

Official notification of implementation should be made by the FS Regional Aviation Officer (RAO) and DOI Aviation Managers through the GACC and, for broader scope implementations, by National Aviation Management through NIFC.

i)   **Phase 2** – Interim Duty Limitations

When Phase 2 is activated, pilots shall adhere to the flight and day-off limitations prescribed in Phase 1 and the duty limitations defined under Phase 2.

(1)   Each flight crew member shall be given an additional day off each fourteen (14) day period. Crews on a twelve (12) and two (2) schedule shall have three (3) consecutive days off (11 and 3). Flight crews on six (6) and one (1) schedules shall work an alternating weekly schedule of five (5) days on, two (2) days off, then six (6) days on and one (1) day off.

(2)   Aircraft fixed daily rates and special rates, when applicable, shall continue to accrue during the extra day off. Contractors may provide additional approved crews to maximize utilization of their aircraft. All costs associated with providing the additional crew will be at the contractor's expense, unless the additional crew is requested by the Government.

ii)   **Phase 3** – Interim Duty Limitations

When Phase 3 is activated, pilots shall adhere to the flight limitations of Phase 1 (standard), the additional day off of Phase 2,   and the limitations defined under Phase 3.

(1)   Flight crew members shall have a minimum of twelve (12) consecutive hours of uninterrupted rest (off duty) during each duty day cycle. The standard duty day shall be no longer than twelve (12) hours, except a crew duty day extension shall not exceed a cumulative fourteen (14) hour duty day. The next flight crew rest period shall then be adjusted to equal the extended duty day, i.e., thirteen (13) hour duty day, thirteen (13) hours rest; fourteen (14) hour duty day, fourteen (14) hours rest. Extended duty day applies only to completion of a mission. In no case may standby be extended beyond the twelve (12) hour duty day.

(2)   Double crews (two (2) complete flight crews assigned to an aircraft), augmented flight crews (an additional pilot-in-command assigned to an aircraft), and aircraft crews that work a rotating schedule, i.e., two (2) days on, one (1) day off, seven (7) days on, seven (7) days off, or twelve (12) days on, twelve (12) days off, may be exempted from Phase 2 Limitations upon verification that their scheduling and duty cycles meet or exceed the provisions of Paragraph a. of Phase 2 and Phase 1 Limitations.

(3) Exemptions based on Paragraph b. of Phase 3 provisions may be requested through the local Aviation Manager or COR, but must be approved by the FS RAO or DOI Area Aviation Manager.

12) Avionics Standards

a) Radio Requirements

Supervision of incident aircraft requires that the ATGS have the minimum capability of monitoring/transmitting on two VHF-FM frequencies, including an Air Guard, which can be continuously monitored, and two VHF-AM frequencies. This allows communications on a primary air- to-air frequency and a secondary air-to-air frequency. The Aerial Supervisor must have the ability to communicate with ground personnel, all tactical logistical aircraft in the incident airspace and the dispatch unit/controlling agency regarding an in-flight emergency/mishap. To meet this requirement USDA-FS or OAS interagency carded aircraft will be equipped with a multi-channel programmable VHF-FM radio system and two multi-channel programmable VHF-AM radios.

i) **Aerial Supervision Aircraft Radio Communications Systems** – As a minimum, the radio system must integrate monitoring and transmitting functions of VHF-AM and VHF-FM systems through the same headphone and microphone. The following table lists avionics standards by type.

Table 3. Interagency Avionics Typing Standards				
Required Avionics Equipment	**Type 1**	**Type 2**	**Type 3**	**Type 4**
Aeronautical VHF-AM radio transceiver	2 each	2 each	2 each	2 each
Aeronautical VHF-FM radio transceiver	2 each	1 each	1 each	
Panel mounted aeronautical GPS	1 each	1 each		
Handheld GPS			1 each	1 each
Separate audio control systems for pilot and ATGS	X	X		
Single audio control system			X	X
Audio/mic jacks with PTT capability in a rear seat connected to co-pilot/ATGS audio control system	X	X		
Intercommunication system	X	X	X	
Plug for auxiliary VHF-FM portable radio or one additional VHF-FM transceiver	X	X		
Accessory Power Source				X
Portable Air Attack Kit				X

(1) **VHF-FM radio(s)** – Must be capable of simultaneously monitoring two frequencies (Narrowband 138 to 174 MHz).

(2) **Air Guard** – (168.625 MHz with transmit tone 110.9) is permanently programmed in the VHF-FM radio. **This frequency must be continuously monitored.**

(3) **Tactical Frequencies** – VHF-FM radio(s) must be capable of storing several tactical frequencies and associated CTCSS tones (if applicable) such as air-to-ground, dispatch, flight following and command.

(4) **National Flight Following** – VHF-FM (168.650 MHz with tx and rx tone of 110.9) is used for point-to-point flight following.

(5) **VHF-AM radio(s)** –Two VHF-AM radios are required (see table above) that monitor 118 to 136.975MHz.

Note: USFS Region 5 and the California Department of Forestry require three VHF-FM and three VHF FM radios in the ATGS aircraft.

b) Minimum Operating Requirements for all Aircraft

At time of dispatch, all aircraft must have both VHF-FM and VHF-AM radio systems in working order. In the event of a radio system failure the following will apply:

i) **Total System Failure** – No ability to monitor or transmit – seek a safe altitude and route and return to base.

ii) **VHF-FM System Failure** – Report problem to other aircraft and dispatch (if able) on VHF-AM system and return to base.

iii) **VHF-AM System Failure** – Report problem to other aircraft, Incident Commander and Dispatch on VHF-FM system and return to base.

c) Frequency Management

Both VHF-FM and VHF-AM frequencies are allocated to wildland agencies. VHF-FM is allocated by the national Telecommunications and Information Administration (NTIA). VHF-AM is allocated by the federal Aviation Administration (FAA). VHF-AM frequencies may change from year to year. Additional FM and AM frequencies may be allocated during major fire emergencies. The agency dispatch centers may order additional frequencies through geographic area coordination centers.

13) Communications Guidelines

a) Flight Following

A VHF-FM frequency is assigned by the dispatch center for check-ins and incident related information. This can be a local unit frequency or the National Flight Following (NFF) frequency (168.650 Tx/Rx. Tone 110.9 Tx/Rx). Some agencies, may assign a VHF-AM flight following frequency. Aircraft flying long distance missions (i.e. cross country) may be required to use the national frequency. Typically, dispatch centers require a 15-minute check in or a confirmation that an aircraft is showing "positive" on the automated flight following (AFF) system. Consult the local dispatch center for local procedures.

b) Air to Ground Communications

It is essential to have a dedicated air-to-ground frequency that is continuously monitored by appropriate ground resources. Tone guarded frequencies should be avoided. The ATGS must always return to air-to-ground after using other VHF-FM frequencies.

i)   **Initial Attack** – Many agencies have pre-assigned FM or AM air-to-ground for different geographic areas. Other agencies use standard work channel frequencies.

ii) **Extended Attack Incidents** – A discreet frequency should be assigned if there are no radio conflicts with other incidents. These frequencies must be ordered through the dispatch system.

(1) **Project (large scale, long term) Incidents** – National Incident Radio Cache (NIICD) radios are programmed with five air tactical frequencies that can be used for air-to-ground communications. Other frequencies can be assigned if there are no radio conflicts with other incidents. These frequencies are assigned by the incident's Communication Unit Leader and are listed in the ICS-220 Air Operations Summary and ICS-205 Incident Radio Communication Plan.

c)   **Air to Air Communications**

Communication between all airborne incident aircraft is critical to safety and effectiveness. Air-to-air communications is usually accomplished using a VHF-AM frequency. California typically uses a VHF-FM for air-to-air communications which requires 3 FM radios to be mounted in the aircraft..

i)   **Primary Air to Air** – The first air-to-air frequency used on an incident is designated as the primary. Agencies may have pre-assigned air-to-air frequencies for initial attack in different geographic areas. Extended attack incidents often require a discreet air-to-air frequency. Project scale incidents have discreet air-to-air frequencies assigned by the incident's Communication Unit Leader that are listed in the ICS-220 (Air Operations Summary) and ICS-205 (Incident Radio Communication Plan).

ii) **Secondary Air to Air** – If needed due to radio congestion, a second air-to-air frequency should be established for helicopter operations. This frequency may also be used for the flight following frequency at the helibase. The ATGS should retain the primary air-to-air frequency for fixed-wing operations so airtankers enroute to the incident can check-in. A discreet air-to-air frequency may be required for Leadplane operations.

iii) **Obtaining Air to Air Frequencies** – Initial and extended attack air-to-air frequencies are obtained through the local dispatch. Project and incident air-to-air frequencies are obtained through the Communications Unit Leader or through the host dispatch center.

iv) **Air to Air Continuity** – The ATGS must maintain continuous air-to-air communications with other incident aircraft. While the Lead and HLCO may use a secondary air-to-air frequency to coordinate their aircraft, the ATGS must communicate with the Lead and HLCO on the primary air-to-air frequency. Air resources under the direct supervision of the ATGS must monitor the primary air-to-air frequency.

d) Air Guard

VHF-FM 168.625 (Tx Tone 110.9) has been established as the USDA/USDI emergency frequency. This frequency is permanently programmed and continuously audible in the multi-channel programmable radio system. Authorized uses of the Air Guard frequency include:

i) In flight aircraft emergencies

ii) Emergency aircraft-to-aircraft communications

iii) Emergency ground-to-aircraft communications

iv) Long range dispatch contact (when use of the designated flight following frequency does not result in contacting dispatch)

v) Initial call, recall, and redirection (divert) of aircraft

e) Air to Air Enroute Position Reporting

During periods of poor visibility a special VHF-AM or FM frequency may be established for inter-aircraft position and altitude reporting enroute to and from or over incidents.

f) Airstrips without Communications

Whenever there is a potential conflict between agency aircraft and public users of back country airstrips, the pilot should announce "in the blind" intentions to land or take off before initiating the maneuver. This is especially important on incidents before air traffic control measures are established.

g) Conflicting Radio Frequencies

When multiple incidents in relatively close proximity (less than 100 miles) are sharing the same tactical frequencies, interference can seriously impair operations. The ATGS must recognize this and request different frequencies through dispatch or the Communications Unit Leader. A local (geographic area) frequency coordinator and the National Incident Radio Support Cache (NIRSC) should be involved when assigning frequencies where several incidents are in close proximity.

h) Tone Guards

Tones have been established by some agencies to allow the use of more frequencies selectively. The tone can be programmed, or selected, in tactical aircraft VHF-FM radios.

i) Air Resource Identifiers

i) ATGS identifier is "Air Attack"

(1) Enroute to/from incident – options include:

(a) Unit name (ex. Wenatchee Air Attack)

(b) Unit assigned identifier (ex. Air Attack 621)

   (c) Aircraft "N" number (ex. Air Attack 81C)

   (d) Working an incident – use incident name (ex. Cougar Air-Attack)

  ii) HLCO identifier is "Helco" or "Copter Coordinator" Apply principles in 1 above (enroute to/from incident).

  iii) The federal ASM identifier is "Bravo", state of Alaska units use "Alpha", and CALFIRE uses "Charlie".

  iv) Lead identifier is "Lead"

   (1) Lead-planes – Pilots are assigned a two-digit identifier (ex. Lead 4-1). CALFIRE Leads use an alpha-numeric designator beginning with C "Charlie" (ex. Lead Charlie 1).

   (2) Lead is used synonymously with the term ATCO

  v) Airtanker: Tanker plus identification number (ex. Tanker 21)

  vi) Helitanker: Helitanker and identification number (ex. Helitanker 42). Applies to Interagency Airtanker Board approved Type 1 fixed tank helicopters

  vii) MAFFS: MAFFS plus identification number (ex. MAFFS 6)

  viii) Helicopter: Copter plus last three characters of N-number (ex. Copter 72 Delta) or a locally assigned agency identifier (ex. Copter 534)

  ix) Smokejumper Aircraft: Jumper plus last two characters of N-number (ex. Jumper 41) or an agency assigned identification number

  x) Other Fixed Wing: Other fixed wing are identified by "make or model prefix" plus last three characters of N-number (ex. Cessna 426)

  xi) Other Identifiers:

   (1) Air Ops: Air Operations Director

   (2) Air Support: Air Support Group Supervisor

   (3) Operations or 'Ops': Operations Section Chief

j) Message Sequence

Protocol requires the resource you are calling be stated first, followed by your identification. "Tanker 23, Trinity Air Attack." Make messages as short and concise as possible

k) Frequency Identification

Monitoring several frequencies sometimes makes it difficult to determine which frequency is being heard. When making initial contact, state the frequency you are transmitting on. "Lead 68, Bear Air Attack on Victor 118.250."

14) Airspace Policy

The *Interagency Airspace Coordination Guide* covers all aspects of wildland agency airspace management. Aerial supervision personnel must be familiar with information in the guide. Dispatch centers and tanker base managers should have a copy available for reference.

a) Federally Designated Special Use Airspace (SUA)

Incidents may be located in, or flight routes to incidents may pass through, areas designated by the Federal Aviation Administration (FAA) as Special Use Areas. Operations through, or within these areas, may require that specific procedures be followed.

Special Use Airspace "consists of airspace wherein activity must be confined because of its nature and/or wherein limitations may be imposed upon aircraft operations that are not part of those activities." These areas include Military Operations Areas (MOA's), Restricted Areas (RA's), Prohibited Areas (PA's) Alert Areas (AA's) Warning Areas (WA's) and Controlled Areas (CFA's).

Special Use Airspace Locations: **All areas except CFA's are identified on NOAA Aeronautical Sectional Charts.** Many of these are located in wildland areas throughout the United States.

Procedures: Appendices 4 and 7 of the *Interagency Airspace Coordination Guide* and the FAA Handbook 7400.2C (Procedures for Handling Airspace Matters) discuss procedures to be used when wildland aerial fire operations are requested in or through these areas. Often, flights through, or within SUA's, require authorization from the using or controlling agencies. Depending on the type of SUA involved, contact with the controlling agency may be initiated by the air resource pilot.

i) **Restricted Areas** – These areas denote the existence of unusual and often invisible hazards to aircraft such as artillery firing, aerial gunnery, or guided missiles. Aircraft must obtain authorization from the controlling agency prior to entry. Many dispatch centers have a de-confliction plan for this type of airspace.

ii) **Military Operations Areas (MOA's)** – Many MOA's in the Western United States are located in airspace over agency lands. Current information regarding MOA scheduling is published in the AP/IA Handbook and Charts. When wildfires occur within these areas, the responsible agency should notify the controlling agency and notify them that incident aircraft will be affected area. Do not assume that there will be no military activity in the area. Authorization is not required to enter a MOA. However, the controlling agency may alter operations in the vicinity of the incident thus increasing the margin of safety.

iii) **Military Training Routes (MTR's)** – MTR's are located over many agency lands in the United States. Some centers should have daily schedule information (hot routes) and may notify the FAA and Military

Scheduling Activity when incident aircraft may conflict with military aircraft on or near the MTR's. Do not assume an MTR has been de-conflicted.

iv) **Other Military Training Routes and Areas** – While the MOA's and MTR's are charted on sectional maps and the AP/IB charts, Slow Speed Low Altitude Training Routes (SR's) and Low Altitude Tactical Navigation Areas (LATN's) and other low altitude flights are not charted and schedules are not published. Dispatch centers should alert you to these flights, if known. The ATGS will notify the dispatch center and other incident aircraft if they observe military aircraft enroute to, near or within the operations area.

b) **Incident Airspace; the Fire Traffic Area (FTA)**

The airspace surrounding an incident is managed by the aerial supervisor who must implement FTA procedures. All wildland incidents, regardless of aircraft on scene, have an FTA. If aerial supervision is not on scene, aircraft will maintain their own separation until aerial supervision arrives.

The FTA is a communication protocol for firefighting agencies. It does not pertain to other aircraft who have legal access within a TFR (Medevac, Law Enforcement, Media, VFR airport traffic, IFR traffic cleared by the FAA.)

Key components and procedures of the FTA include:

i) **Initial Contact Ring** – A ring 12nm from the center point of the incident. At this point, inbound aircraft contact the ATGS or appropriate aerial resource for permission to proceed to the incident. Briefing information is provided to the inbound aircraft by the aerial supervision resource over the incident (ATGS, ATCO, ASM, and HLCO).

ii) **No Communication (NOCOM) Ring** – A ring 7nm from the center point of the incident that should not be crossed by inbound aircraft without first establishing communications with the appropriate aerial supervision resource.

iii) **Three (3) C's of initial contact** – Communication requirements and related actions to be undertaken by the pilot of the inbound aircraft:

(1) **Communication** – Establish communications with the controlling aerial supervision resource over the incident. (ATGS, ATCO, ASM, HLCO).

(2) **Clearance** – Receive clearance from aerial supervision resource to proceed to the incident past the NOCOM ring. Inbound pilot will acknowledge receipt of clearance or (hold) outside the NOCOM ring until the clearance is received and understood.

(3) **Comply** – Inbound aircraft will comply with clearance from aerial supervision resource. If compliance cannot be accomplished, the inbound aircraft will remain outside the NOCOM ring until an amended clearance is received and understood.

iv) **Departing Aircraft** – Aircraft departing incident airspace must communicate their intentions to aerial supervision to obtain a safe departure route to their destination. Aircraft (especially helicopters) often recover to multiple bases, fuel sites or other offsite landing areas. Aerial Supervisors/Pilots must establish/de-conflict routes for departing aircraft through or away from other incident aircraft operations.

Figure 4. Fire Traffic Area

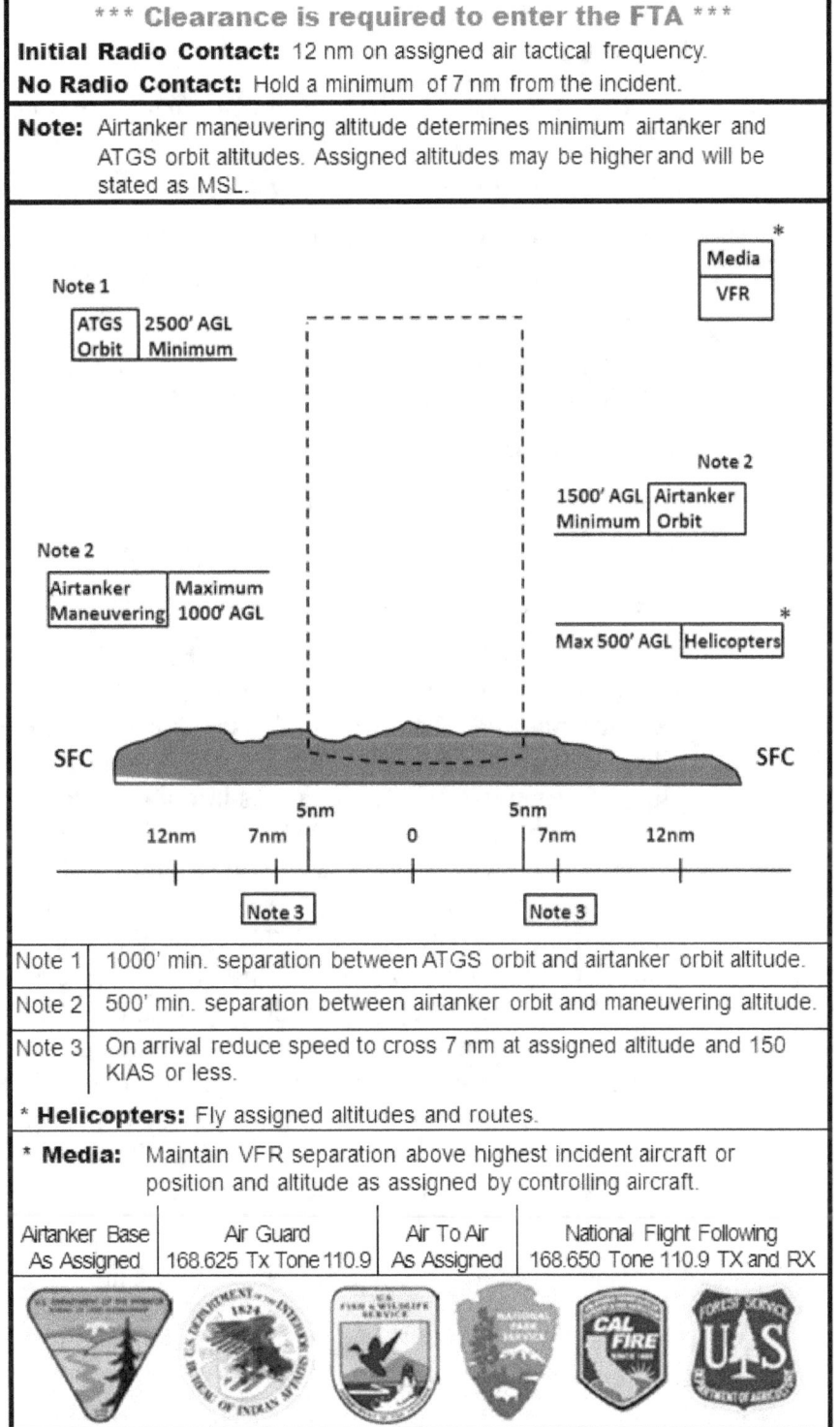

Fire Traffic Area (FTA)   01 May 2013

*** Clearance is required to enter the FTA ***

Initial Radio Contact: 12 nm on assigned air tactical frequency.
No Radio Contact: Hold a minimum of 7 nm from the incident.

Note: Airtanker maneuvering altitude determines minimum airtanker and ATGS orbit altitudes. Assigned altitudes may be higher and will be stated as MSL.

Note 1 — ATGS Orbit | 2500' AGL Minimum

Media VFR *

Note 2 — 1500' AGL Minimum | Airtanker Orbit

Note 2 — Airtanker Maneuvering | Maximum 1000' AGL

Max 500' AGL | Helicopters *

SFC — SFC

12nm 7nm 5nm 0 5nm 7nm 12nm

Note 3   Note 3

Note 1	1000' min. separation between ATGS orbit and airtanker orbit altitude.
Note 2	500' min. separation between airtanker orbit and maneuvering altitude.
Note 3	On arrival reduce speed to cross 7 nm at assigned altitude and 150 KIAS or less.

* Helicopters: Fly assigned altitudes and routes.

* Media: Maintain VFR separation above highest incident aircraft or position and altitude as assigned by controlling aircraft.

| Airtanker Base As Assigned | Air Guard 168.625 Tx Tone 110.9 | Air To Air As Assigned | National Flight Following 168.650 Tone 110.9 TX and RX |

National Interagency Airspace: http://airspacecoordination.org

c) **Temporary Flight Restriction (TFR)**

Under the conditions listed below the responsible agency should request a temporary flight restriction under FAR Part 91.137. A TFR may be initiated by the dispatch center, Incident Commander, Air Operations Branch Director, Lead, ASM, or ATGS.

For more information, refer to Chapter 6 of the *Interagency Airspace Coordination Guide*.

i) **Considerations for Requesting a TFR-FAR Part 91.137**

(1) Length of operation: Extended operations (>3 hours) are anticipated. Local agency policy for the anticipated length of incident operations may apply.

(2) Congested airspace involved: Operations are in the vicinity of high-density civil aircraft operation (airports).

(3) Incident size and complexity

(4) Potential conflict with non-operational aircraft

(5) Extended operations on Military Training Routes

(6) Extended Operations within Special Use Airspace

(7) **Aerial Supervision Responsibility & TFRs** – During the initial attack phase of an incident, the aerial supervisor may initiate a request for a TFR. The aerial supervisor should complete critical information required on the Interagency Request for Temporary Flight Restriction form and radio this information to the responsible dispatch coordination center. On Type 1 or 2 incidents, the ATGS in consultation with the Lead or ASM, will advise the Air Operations Branch Director when the dimensions of the TFR should be increased or decreased. These changes must be forwarded immediately to the dispatch center that will initiate a new order to the FAA. The aerial supervisor should coordinate with the incident Air Operations Branch Director or local dispatch office as appropriate to recommend termination of an existing TFR. Aerial supervision aircraft not assigned to the incident must stay clear of TFRs unless communication is established with the controlling entity (ATGS, ASM, Leadplane, etc) and authorization is given to enter the TFR.

(8) Ordering a TFR – Three pieces of information are required:

(a) Center point in DMS format

(b) Vertical dimension in feet MSL

(c) Horizontal radius in NM from center point

(d) Non-standard/non circular TFR dimensions require points in DMS format at each corner of the polygon.

ii) **Guidelines for TFR Dimensions** – The *Interagency Airspace Coordination Guide* covers this subject in detail. Factors which must be considered are:

(1) The type and number of aircraft operations occurring within the incident airspace and their aeronautical requirements

(2) The operating altitude to provide the ATGS a safe and good vantage point

(3) Entry and exit points and routes

(4) Other aircraft operations in the geographical area

(5) Size, shape and rate of increase of the incident

(6) Location of incident helibases, water sources, etc

(7) Location of commercial airports

iii) **TFR Lateral Dimensions**: Normally 5 nautical miles radius from center point of the incident/project. Any aircraft operating base within "reasonable distance" should be included (helibase, heli-dip site). Lateral dimensions may be much greater on large incidents. The lateral dimensions/shape may be irregular to conform to actual requirements. Dimensions should be no more than you need.

iv) **TFR Vertical Dimensions** – In general, the airspace should extend up to (but not include) an elevation of 2000 ft. above the highest terrain (above ground level) *or 2000 ft. above the highest-flying aircraft on the incident.* The vertical and lateral dimensions of the desired airspace may conflict with FAA requirements and what they will approve. The FAA, through the dispatch center, will provide the approved TFR dimensions. If airspace needs are not met, request new air space dimensions. Again, the adjusted airspace requires FAA approval.

v) **TFRs for Multiple Incidents In Close Proximity** – Multiple incidents in close proximity may result in overlapping restrictions. To avoid confusion the respective dispatchers and Air Operations Branch Directors should consolidate multiple TFR's into one manageable TFR.

vi) **Proper Identification of TFR Part 91.137 Paragraph** – TFR Part 91.137 is divided into three sections referred to as Paragraphs (a)(1), (a)(2), and (a)(3) indicating the type of disaster event normally associated with each designation. The most commonly requested TFR for wildfire is 91.137 (a)(2).

(a)(1) – Volcanic eruption, toxic gas leaks, spills.

(a)(2) – Forest and range fires.

(a)(3) – Incidents/events generating high public interest such as sporting events.

vii) **Non-Incident Aircraft TFR Policy**:

14 CFR 91.137 (a) 2 prescribes how Temporary Flight Restrictions are established to provide a safe environment for the operation of disaster relief aircraft. When a NOTAM has been issued under this CFR section, all aircraft are prohibited from operating in the designated area unless at least one of the following conditions is met:

(1) "The aircraft is participating in hazard relief activities and is being operated under the direction of the official in charge of on-scene emergency response activities."

(2) "The aircraft is carrying **law enforcement** officials."

(3) "The aircraft is operating under the **ATC approved IFR flight plan**."

(4) "The operation is conducted **directly to or from an airport** within the area, or is necessitated by the impracticability of VFR flight above or around the area due to weather, or terrain; notification is given to the Flight Service Station (FSS) or **ATC facility** specified in the NOTAM to receive advisories concerning disaster relief aircraft operations; and the operation does not hamper or endanger relief activities and is not conducted for observing the disaster."

(5) "The aircraft is carrying **properly accredited news representatives**, and prior to entering the area, a flight plan is filed with the appropriate FAA or ATC facility specified in the Notice to Airmen and the operation is conducted above the altitude used by the disaster relief aircraft, unless otherwise authorized by the official in charge of on scene emergency response activities."

Note: According to FAA JO7210.3X *"Coordination with the official in charge of on-scene emergency response activities is required prior to ATC allowing any IFR or VFR aircraft to enter into the TFR area."* The FAA Advisory Circular 91-63C states *"Notification must be given to the ATC/Flight Service Station (FSS) specified in the NOTAM for coordination with the official in charge of on-scene emergency response activities."*

Some accommodations (for flights such as early morning agricultural spraying operations) can be made through the establishment of time specific Temporary Flight Restrictions that releases the airspace for use after hours.

With no legal authority to waive 14 CFR 91.137 and allow nonparticipating aviation, which do not meet at least one of the access criteria identified on page 1, to "pass through" the TFR area, ATGS, ASM and HLCO have only two options: 1.) Release the TFR (through normal ordering channels) to accommodate the requests 2.) **Advise the requestor that they will have to continue to fly around the TFR for their own safety.**

d) Air Operations in Congested Areas

Airtankers can drop retardant in congested areas under DOI authority given in FAR Part 137. FS authority is granted in exemption 392, FAR 91.119 as referenced in FSM 9714. When such are necessary, they may be authorized subject to these limitations:

i)   Airtanker operations in congested areas may be conducted at the request of the city, rural fire department, county, state, or federal fire suppression agency.

ii) An ASM or Leadplane is ordered to coordinate aerial operations.

iii) The air traffic control facility responsible for the airspace is notified prior to or as soon as possible after the beginning of the operation.

iv) A positive communication link must be established between the airtanker coordinator or the aerial supervision module (ASM), airtanker pilots, and the responsible fire suppression agency official.

v)   The IC or designee for the responsible agency will advise aerial supervision personnel or airtanker that the line is clear before retardant drops.

e) Use of Firefighting Aircraft Transponder Code 1255

All incident aircraft will utilize a transponder code of 1255 unless another code is assigned by air traffic control.

f) Responses to Airspace Conflicts and Intrusions

When incident airspace conflicts and intrusions occur the aerial supervisor must:

i)   Immediately ensure the safety of incident aircraft.

ii) Notify incident aircraft in the immediate area of the position of the intruder.

iii) Attempt radio contact with intruder aircraft by use of VHF-AM (known Victor, local unicom) and VHF-FM (assigned, local, or Air Guard) frequencies.

iv) If radio contact can be established, inform the intruder of the incident in progress, airspace restriction limitations in effect, and other aircraft in the area. Determine if the intruder has legitimate authority to be within the TFR.

v)   Request intruder depart restricted area (assign an altitude and heading if necessary). Request the intruder to stay in radio contact until clear of the area.

vi) If the aircraft is a legitimate "non-participating" aircraft and has the authority to be within the area, communicate with the aircraft and advise incident aircraft of its presence. If possible, coordinate altitudes and locations. The ATGS may request, but not demand that the aircraft check in with the ATGS as needed. If radio contact is not established:

(1) No attempt to drive, guide or force the intruder from the area should be made. The aerial supervisor must monitor intruder's position, altitude, and heading.

(2) Try to ascertain the N-number without imposing a hazard.

(3) The aerial supervisor must ensure that incident aircraft are informed and kept clear of intruder. This may require removing incident aircraft and curtailing operations for as long as intruder is considered a potential hazard.

(4) Report intruder immediately to local dispatch office and ask them to contact the Air Route Traffic Control Center (ARTCC). The FAA sometimes has the capability of tracking an aircraft or identifying the aircraft.

vii) If there is a conflict or intrusion, report it to the appropriate dispatch center. Ask dispatch to report the intrusion the local ARTCC.

viii) Submit a Mishap or SAFECOM Report as per agency policy and procedures.

g) **Special Use Airspace Reminders**

i) Check with dispatch when receiving the Resource Order.

ii) Is the incident in SUA?

iii) Is the Restricted Area/MOA/MTR "hot" or about to be?

iv) Confirm military has been notified and what action will be taken.

v) The pilot must obtain clearance/routing through or around restricted areas enroute to the incident.

vi) Always be alert for military aircraft even when SUA/MTRs are "cold."

h) **Canadian Airtankers on U.S. Border Fires**

On fires near the Canadian/U.S. border, a Canadian Air Attack Group may be dispatched to a U.S. fire.

i) Normally this group includes two scooping tankers and a Bird Dog.

ii) On board the Bird Dog is an Air Attack Officer, very similar to an ATGS.

iii) Typically on a 'quick strike' across the border, the Bird Dog would assume control of the airspace and work the fire until/unless an ATGS is present

iv) When a U.S. ATGS is on scene, the ATGS has overall responsibility for the airspace. The Bird Dog is in charge of directing Canadian Airtanker operations much like a Leadplane under the supervision of the ATGS.

The ATGS is responsible for the direction of all U.S. resources and the Bird Dog.

v) Refer to policies of the local agency or your home agency with regard to utilization of Canadian air resources.

vi) The local unit Dispatch should coordinate flights with Air and Marine Interdiction Coordination Center at 1-866-AIRBUST.

This page intentionally left blank.

Chapter 5 – Incident Aircraft

Aerial supervisors should have knowledge of the types of aircraft they supervise, how to communicate with them, and the logistics required to support them.

Tactical and logistical aircraft supervised and coordinated by aerial supervisors may be procured from the USDA Forest Service, USDI Aviation Management Directorate, US Department of Defense, or state, county or municipal sources. Contract or procurement agreement requirements and standards will vary among the various sources. For more detailed information about air tactical and logistical aircraft, refer to the Aircraft Identification Library on the DOI/FS Interagency Aviation Training site at https://www.iat.gov/aircraft_library/.

1) Airtankers

The Incident Command System (ICS) recognizes four categories or types of airtankers based on gallons retardant/suppressant capability. Type 1, 2 and 3 airtankers listed below have been evaluated and approved by the Interagency Airtanker Board. Type 4 airtankers are airtankers (SEATs) with less than an 800-gallon capacity and have been approved by the Department of the Interior.

Table 4. Airtanker Classification

(does not account for retardant download requirements)

Aircraft	Maximum Gallons	Cruise Speed (knots)	Number of Doors
Very Large Airtanker (VLAT)			
DC-10	12,000	280	3 Constant Flow Tanks
Type 1: 3,000 Minimum Gallon Capacity			
C-130 (MAFFS)	3000	250	1- Pressurized System
P3-A	3000	240	1- Constant Flow
DC-7	3000	235	6-8
BAE-146 and RJ series	3,000	330	1 - Variable Flow
Type 2: 1800-2999 Gallon Capacity			
DC-6	2,450	215	8
P2-V	2,450	184	6
Type 3: 800-1,799 Gallon Capacity			
CL-215 (Scooper)	1,400 (Water)	160	2 (foam capable)
CL-415 (Scooper)	1,600 (Water)	180	4 (foam capable)
S2 Tracker	800	180	4
S2 Turbine Tracker	1,200	230	Constant Flow
Air Tractor AT-802 F	800	170	Constant Flow
Type 4: Less than 800 Gallons			
Air Tractor AT-802/602	600-799	160 mph	1 (in-line or horizontal)
Turbine Thrush	400-770	140 mph	1 (in-line or horizontal)
Turbine Dromader	500	140 mph	1 (in-line or horizontal)
Piston Dromader	500	115 mph	1 (in-line or horizontal)

a) **Airtanker Retardant Delivery Systems**

Due to the number of approved airtanker makes/models and the number of airtanker operators there are several approved tank/door systems. The tank/door systems are now evaluated and approved by the Interagency Airtanker Board to ensure that the systems meet desired coverage level and drop characteristics. The four basic systems used today include the following:

i) **Variable Tank Door System** – Multiple tanks or compartments controlled by an electronic intervalometer control mechanism to open doors singly, simultaneously or in an interval sequence. The pilot may select a low flow rate or a high flow rate.

ii) **Constant Rate System** – A single compartment with two doors controlled by a computer. The system is capable of single or multiple even flow drops at designated coverage levels from .5 GPC to +8 GPC.

iii) **Pressurized Tank System** – Modular Airborne Fire Fighting Systems (MAFFS) C-130s are equipped with a pressurized system to discharge their 3,000 gallons of retardant through two 18-inch tubes. General coverage levels can be obtained by regulating pressure/PSI settings. A few of the MAFFS units are capable of incremental drops of 1000 or 2000 gallons. The maximum flow rate produces a coverage level 4 (4GPC).

iv) **Standard Tank System** – This system is common on SEATs. Single or multiple tanks/compartments controlled manually or electronically. Some tank systems may be controlled by an electronic intervalometer control mechanism to open doors singly, simultaneously or in an interval sequence.

b) **Helicopters**

ICS categorizes three types of helicopters based on minimum gallons of water/retardant, lift capability, number of passenger seats, and pound card weight capacity. Operations personnel refer to helicopters by type. Density altitude will greatly affect lift capability. Loads under high density altitude conditions are displayed in the helicopter classification table.

Table 5. Helicopter Classification		
Aircraft	Typical Payload at 8000' Density Altitude	Typical Payload at 11,000' Density Altitude
Type 1 (Heavy)		
Sikorsky S-64E (Aircrane)	12,700	9,117
Sikorsky S-64F (Aircrane)	15,640	10,288
Boeing 234 (Chinook)	19,063	15,363
Boeing 107 (Vertol)	4,656	3,424
Sikorsky S-61	4,038	2,221
Bell B-214	3,754	2,665
Aerospatiale 332L (Super Puma)	4,328	2,729
Aerospatiale 330 (Puma)	4,525	3,325
Kaman 1200 (Kmax)	5,288	4,588
Sikorsky CH-54 or CH-64 (Skycrane)	11,098	7,978
Sikorsky S-70 (Firehawk)	6,569	5,669
Type 2 Helicopters (Medium)		
Bell B-212	1,973	1,010
Bell B-205A-1	1,294	642
Bell B-205A-1+	1,596	896
Bell B-205A-1++ (Super 205)	2,806	2,120
Bell B-412	1,742	884
Sikorsky S-58T	1,635	597
Type 3 Helicopters (Light)		
Aerospatiale 315B (Llama)	925	925
Bell B-206 B3 (Jet Ranger)	715	380
Bell B-206 L3 (Long Ranger)	950	830
Bell B-206 L4 (Long Ranger)	1,196	767
Bell B-407	1,315	880
Aerospatiale 350-B2 (Astar)	1,083	700
Aerospatiale 350-B3 (Astar)	1,972	1,911
Hughes 500 D	515	295

i) **Helicopter Retardant/Suppressant Delivery Systems** – There are two basic delivery systems: bucket and tank systems.

(1) **Buckets** – Two types of helicopter buckets are used. These include:

(a) Rigid Shell (100 to 3,000 gallons)

(b) Collapsible (94-2000 gallons)

(2) **Tanks** – Internal and external tank systems have been developed for various Type 1-3 helicopters. These include:

(a) Computerized metered or constant flow tank system

(b) Conventional tank/door system

Note: Heavy helicopters with fixed tanks are referred to as "helitankers"

c) **Leadplane and ASM Aircraft**

Airplanes utilized for Leadplane operations are typically twin engine turboprop aircraft such as the King Air 90 or Commander 600 series. The state of Alaska utilizes a single engine turboprop; the Pilatus PC-7.

d) **ATGS Aircraft**

Both high wing, single or twin engine airplanes and Type 3 helicopters make suitable ATGS aircraft depending on mission requirements. Each has its advantages and disadvantages.

Table 6. Common ATGS Aircraft					
Make/Model	*PAX*	*Payload (lbs)*	*Wing Config*	*Engines/Type*	*Cruise Speed (kts)*
Cessna 182	3	600	High	1 - Piston	135
Cessna 206	5	900	High	1 - Piston	135
Cessna 337	3	600	High	2 - Piston	148
Commander 500 series	5	900	High	2 - Piston	169
Cessna 340	5	900	Low	2 - Piston	182
Commander 600 series	5-11	1,250	High	2 - Turbine	185

In selecting an ATGS aircraft for a particular assignment, the following should be considered:

i) **Visibility**

(1) Fixed-Wing

(a) High or low wing aircraft designed with the cockpit forward of the wings typically good visibility

(b) Low wing aircraft designed with the cockpit over the wings; provide for limited visibility

(2)   Helicopters: Open cockpit designs facilitate excellent visibility

ii)   **Speed** – For large, initial attack, and multiple incident scenarios, aircraft speed is important. On initial attack incidents in particular, it is key that the ATGS arrive before other aerial resources in order to determine incident objectives and set up the airspace. Twin-engine fixed-wing aircraft are usually the best choice in these situations (150+ knots cruise speed with 200+ knots desirable).

    (1)   Twin-Engine Fixed Wing – Fast (generally greater than 150 kts)

    (2)   Single-Engine Fixed Wing – Slower (generally less than 150 kts)

    (3)   Helicopters – Slowest (generally less than 130 kts)

iii)   **Maneuverability** – It is essential that the aircraft can be positioned for the particular mission observation requirements. Helicopters are excellent for target identification and for monitoring and evaluating mission effectiveness. A Type 3 helicopter is generally the best platform for a helicopter coordinator.

iv)   **Economics** – Aircraft costs must be reasonable and commensurate with the cost-benefit to a particular incident.

    (1)   Single-Engine Fixed Wing – Least expensive

    (2)   Twin-Engine Fixed Wing – More expensive

    (3)   Helicopters – Most expensive

v)   **Noise level** – Excessive noise can interfere with the ability to communicate for prolonged periods of time and can contribute to fatigue. Consider use of an active noise-canceling headset to help mitigate noise related fatigue.

    (1)   Single-Engine Fixed Wing – Highest cockpit noise level

    (2)   Twin-Engine Fixed Wing – Less cockpit noise level

    (3)   Helicopters – Least cockpit noise level (flight helmet is required)

vi)   **Base of Operations** – Airport facilities, distance from the incident base and distance from the dispatch center are considerations in determining the best base of operations.

vii)   **Initial Attack Incidents** – It is generally best to be co-located with airtankers and Leadplanes at an airtanker base to facilitate briefings. It may be desirable to be located near a dispatch center for the same reason.

viii)   **Large Incidents** – It may be desirable to be located at or near the incident to facilitate briefing and de-briefing with the Operations Section.

ix)   **Airstrip Considerations**

    (1)   **Single-Engine Fixed Wing** – Can generally operate from shorter airstrips than twin engine airplanes.

(2) **Twin-Engine Fixed Wing** – Require longer runways and usually require an improved surface.

(3) **Helicopters** – Helicopters are advantageous if the incident is not near any airport and if it is critical for the ATGS to meet with the Operations Section Chief. It may also be desirable for the ATGS, Operations Section Chief and Division Group Supervisor(s) to fly reconnaissance missions in the same aircraft.

x) **Cabin space** – Mission requirements may necessitate the need for an observer or an Air Tactical trainee/instructor in addition to minimum flight crew requirements.

xi) **Safety** – Consider performance capability of the aircraft for the density altitude and terrain at which operations are conducted.

xii) **Aircraft and Pilot Approvals** – Aircraft must have interagency approval to be used for an air tactical mission. The approval card must be carried onboard the aircraft. Similarly, pilots used for air tactical missions must possess a current approval card.

xiii) **Avionics Equipment** – In addition to the above avionics requirements, the following are typically required:

(1) Headset(s) with boom microphones

(2) Voice Activated Intercom

(3) Separate Audio Panels for the pilot and ATGS/ATS

(4) Separate volume and squelch controls for the pilot and ATGS/ATS

(5) A separate audio panel and voice activated intercom station in a rear seat may be required in aircraft to accommodate an ATGS/ATS trainee (observer) of ATGS instructor or check airman

xiv) **Traffic Collision Avoidance System (TCAS/TCAD)** – The threat of midair collision is ever present in the fire environment. TCAS/TCAD is now part of the standard equipment in Leadplanes and ASM aircraft. The systems are enhanced with special features designed to improve safety and operational effectiveness on incidents. USFS Smokejumper airplanes are equipped with TCAS.

e) **Helicopter Coordinator Aircraft**

A Type 3 helicopter is generally used by the Helicopter Coordinator.

f) **Smokejumper Aircraft**

Smokejumper aircraft are turbine-powered medium to heavy aircraft carrying 8 to 18 smokejumpers plus spotters and flight crew. Smokejumpers are primarily used for initial attack but are also used to reinforce large fires, build helispots, etc. Examples include the Twin Otter, Sherpa, Casa, turbine DC-3, and Dornier.

Table 7. Smokejumper Aircraft				
Aircraft	Cruise Speed (kts)	Cruise Speed (mph)	Range (statute miles)	Jumpers
Turbine DC-3	190	220	1000	12–18
Sherpa	170	195	600	10
Twin Otter	150	170	500	8
Casa 212	170	195	500	8
Dornier	200	230	750	8

g) **Modular Airborne Firefighting System (MAFFS)**

i) **Policy**: The National Interagency Coordination Center (NICC) mobilizes

Modular Airborne Firefighting Systems (MAFFS) as a reinforcement measure when suitable contract airtankers are not readily available within the contiguous 48 states.

MAFFS may be made available to assist foreign governments when requested through the State Department or other diplomatic memorandums of understanding.

The Governors of California, North Carolina and Wyoming may activate MAFFS units for missions within State boundaries under their respective memorandums of understanding with military authorities and the Forest Service. Approval from the Forest Service Director, NIFC is required prior to activation.

Through the Memorandum of Understanding the USDA, Forest Service will provide the following resources:

(1) MAFFS unit "slip-in tank" systems.

(2) Qualified MAFFS Leadplane Pilot.

(3) MAFFS Liaison Officer (MLO).

(4) MAFFS Airtanker Base Manager (MABM).

(5) VHF-FM radios.

ii) **MAFFS Aircraft Locations** – Air National Guard and Air Force Reserve units utilizing C-130 are based at the following locations:

(1) Charlotte, North Carolina (145th AW) – Air National Guard

(2) Port Hueneme, California (146th AW) – Air National Guard

(3) Cheyenne, Wyoming (153rd AW– Air National Guard

(4) Colorado Springs, Colorado (302nd AW) – Air Force Reserve

iii) **Training and Proficiency** – Training will be conducted by the Forest Service, National MAFFS Training Coordinator annually for military and agency personnel. Specific training dates will be negotiated with the military airlift wings.

iv) **MAFFS Leadplane Pilot** – Agency Leadplane Pilots must participate every 4 years to be re-qualified for operations with MAFFS. Qualified MAFFS Leadplane Pilots will be listed in the *National Interagency Mobilization Guide*.

v) **MAFFS Flight Crews** – Training of MAFFS crews will be in accordance with military qualifications and continuation training requirements. To become qualified to fly MAFFS operations, MAFFS flight crews must attend initial and recurrent training as appropriate at the annual MAFFS training session. The AFMC will certify to the Forest Service National MAFFS Training Coordinator. The status of flight crewmembers at the completion of the annual training currency requirements are as follows:

(1) MAFFS airdrop currency is required annually. If more than 120 days has elapsed since the last air drop, the crew's first air drop will be restricted to a target judged by the MAFFS Leadplane Pilot to offer the fewest hazards.

(2) If more than 8 months have elapsed since the last MAFFS air drop, an airborne MAFFS Leadplane Pilot supervised water drop will be required before entering the incident area.

(3) Currency training will be conducted by the National MAFFS Training Coordinator annually. Specific training dates will be negotiated with each airlift wing.

vi) **MAFFS Operations Policies**

(1) **MAFFS aircraft identification** – Each MAFFS aircraft will be identified by a large, high visibility number on the aircraft tail, side of the fuselage aft of the cockpit area, and on top the fuselage cabin. The MAFFS call sign will be this number (i.e., MAFFS 2).

(2) **Supervision of a MAFFS Mission**

(a) No MAFFS mission will be flown unless under the supervision of a qualified MAFFS Leadplane Pilot. The Leadplane Pilot will communicate with the MLO/AFMC daily on flight needs of military crews.

(b) International MAFFS missions will utilize a qualified MAFFS Leadplane Pilot in the MAFFS aircraft to assist the Aircraft Commander with tactical requirements. Headquarters (HQ) Military Airlift Command (MAC) approval must be obtained prior to flying civilian personnel aboard MAFFS aircraft.

(c) Lead operations will be provided on each run and the runs are restricted to one MAFFS aircraft at a time with no daisy-chain operations of multiple aircraft in trail.

(d) Leadplane pilot trainees will not function as the Leadplane Pilot (LP) on MAFFS operations. If the trainee is in the left seat, the LP Instructor will fly the run from the right seat.

(3) **Military Flight Duty Limitations**

(a) Flight time will not exceed a total of 8 hours per day.

(b) A normal duty day is limited to 12 hours.

(c) Within any 24-hour period, pilots shall have a minimum of 12 consecutive hours off duty immediately prior to the beginning of any duty day.

(d) Duty includes flight time, ground duty of any kind, and standby or alert status at any location.

vii) **Standard Operating Procedures** – Procedures for "working" MAFFS on an incident are the same as for contract airtankers. MAFFS flight crews are rotated on a regular basis. The AFMC will verify the status of the flight crews with the MLO. Leadplane Pilots should be aware that newly rotated flight crews may have restrictions on their initial air drops to accomplish currency requirements.

viii) **Operational Considerations** – The procedures for using MAFFS over an incident are the much the same as those used for contract airtankers. The ATGS should be aware of the following "key" differences when using MAFFS aircraft:

(1) **Volume** – C-130s configured with MAFFS 2 (M2) normally carry 3000 gallons unless takeoff performance requires a download.

(2) **Load Portions** – Drops may be divided in to FULL, half, 1/3^{rd,} and 1/6th

(3) **Coverage Levels** – M2 is capable of Coverage Levels 1, 2, 3, 4, 6, and 8.

(4) **Retardant Line Width** – M2 has a narrower but more uniform line pattern than commercial airtankers. This is a characteristic of the nozzle on the pressurized system. Density (coverage level) at the center meets IAB criteria and remains consistent along the path of delivery.

(5) **Reload** – M2 can be sent to reload at pre-approved bases identified in the IAT Base Directory MAFFS Supplement. Normally, following the final air drop MAFFS aircraft will recover to the activation base for servicing by military personnel.

ix) **Communications Considerations**

(1) **Aircraft Identifier** – The number displayed on the aircraft fuselage will identify MAFFS aircraft.

(2) **Radio Hardware** – MAFFS aircraft are equipped with one Forest Service supplied P-25 compliant VHF-FM radio operating over the frequency band of 138 -174 MHz. Communications may also be conducted using a VHF-AM frequency in the 118-136.975 MHz bandwidth in the same manner as other contract air tactical resources.

(3) **Check in Procedure** – The ATGS (or LEAD/ASM) in the absence of an ATGS) must identify the location and altitude of all other aircraft operating over the incident as well as the incident altimeter setting to all MAFFS aircraft 'checking in' enroute to the incident.

(4) **Dispatch Communications** – The ATGS or Lead will notify dispatch whether additional loads of retardant will be required to meet operational objectives on the incident.

h) **Military Helicopter Operations**

Regular Military refers to active military, reserve units and "federalized" National Guard aviation assets. For an in depth discussion of military helicopter operations, refer to Chapter 70 of the Military Use Handbook (2001). Key portions of the parent text are included below.

i) **Policy**: Regular military helicopter assets may be provided by the Department of Defense – Support of Civilian Authority as requested by appropriate ordering entities when civilian aviation resources are depleted.

ii) **Mission Profiles** – Mission profiles for regular military helicopter units are normally limited to:

(1) Reconnaissance or Command and Control activities

(2) Medevac

(3) Crew transportation

(4) Cargo transportation (internal and external loads)

(5) Crew and cargo staging from airports to base camps for incident support

iii) **Bucket Operations** – Occasionally conducted with regular military helicopters. If bucket operations are conducted, a Helicopter Coordinator (HLCO) shall be utilized whenever regular military helicopters are engaged in bucket operations.

iv) **Communications**

(1) Military Radio Hardware – Regular military aircraft are equipped with VHF-AM aeronautical radios that operate in the 118 to 136.975 MHz bandwidth.

(2) **Agency Provided Radio Hardware** – VHF-FM aeronautical transceivers compatible with agency frequencies may be provided by the agency.

Note: Until agency furnished VHF-FM radio systems can be installed, a Helicopter Coordinator (HLCO) is required. Multi-ship operations may be conducted without a Helicopter Coordinator if at least one helicopter has compatible communications capability with civilian bandwidths.

i) **National Guard Helicopter Operations**

i) **Policy**: The use of National Guard helicopters for federal firefighting purposes within their state boundaries is addressed in applicable regional, State or local agreements or memorandums of understanding between federal agencies and specific National Guard units. The aerial supervisor should coordinate with local agency officials, agency aviation management specialists or the Air Operations Branch Director to ensure planned use of National Guard assets complies with applicable policy and procedures specific to the local area and/or participating jurisdictions.

ii) **Mobilization Authority** – The Governor can mobilize National Guard aviation assets at the request of local or State jurisdictions for incidents on private land or multi-jurisdictional incidents.

iii) **Mission Profiles** – In addition to the mission profiles discussed for regular military helicopters above, National Guard helicopters routinely engage in water bucket operations in many States.

iv) **Communications and HLCO** – Lack of VHF-FM communications capability may be a problem to be addressed prior to use of National Guard aviation assets on federal or multi-jurisdictional incidents. Use of a Helicopter Coordinator (HLCO) should be considered to mitigate communications issues with ground and aviation resources on an incident.

v) **Training & Proficiency Assessment** – Operational procedures, mission training, and proficiency vary between States, National Guard units and flight crews. The ATGS should assess the proficiency of the resource and make adjustments as appropriate to provide for the safe and effective use of National Guard resources.

j) **Water Scooping Aircraft**

Canadair CL-21, 415, and AT-802 Fireboss

i) **Policy and Availability**

(1) **United States** – Water scooping aircraft are located or utilized in the states of Minnesota, North Carolina, Alaska, California, and the northwestern area. Besides working in their home states, it is likely that these aircraft will be encountered elsewhere in the U.S. under

contract or on a call-when-needed (CWN) basis where water sources are conducive to operations.

(2) **Canada** – Water scooping aircraft are widely used in Canada, especially from Quebec west to Alberta. States bordering Canada may have agreements such as the Great Lakes Compact that outline procedures for sharing resources on fires within a specified distance from the border. There may also be provisions for extended use of Canadian Airtankers in the U.S. when needed and if available. Aerial supervisors should obtain a briefing on these agreements or procedures when assigned, if applicable.

k) Firewatch Aerial Supervision Platforms

The USFS Firewatch Aerial Supervision Helicopter is a Bell 209 Cobra Helicopter converted for use by the US Forest Service for use as an aerial supervision and intelligence gathering platform. There are currently two platforms in use in Region 5, Air Attack 507 and Air Attack 509. The platforms are statused as Initial Attack ATGS platforms based in Redding (AA-507) and Lancaster (509). **The platforms are staffed daily with a qualified Bell 209 Pilot and a qualified ATGS.**

i) **Call Signs** – For mission clarification:

(1) When in the ATGS profile the Firewatch Aerial Supervision Helicopter will use the call sign "Air Attack 507 (509)".

(2) When performing the HLCO mission, the call sign is "HLCO" or "HLCO 509 (507)".

(3) For intelligence gathering, mapping or suppression resource support profile, the Firewatch Aerial Supervision Platform will use the call sign "Firewatch 507 (509)".

ii) **Mission Profiles** – The USFS Firewatch Helicopter will request entry into the fire traffic area in one of the following mission profiles:

(1) **Tactical**

(a) ATGS

(b) HLCO

(c) Crew/suppression resource intelligence support

Clearance for the Firewatch Platform (AA 507 or 509) into the Fire Traffic Area as an ATGS or HLCO should be the same as any relief or initial attack ATGS or HLCO clearance, one thousand feet either above or below the on scene Aerial Supervision or controlling platform for initial briefing and transition of control.

When in the Crew / Suppression Resource Intelligence Support profile, the Firewatch Platform may request low level, 500 AGL and below for direct crew support. If performing a live video feed for the ground forces, the Firewatch Platform may request varying altitudes for better "big picture" video feed. Work the Cobra into the traffic patterns as any direct suppression aircraft. The Firewatch Platform may also request an offsite landing to pass the portable downlink receiver ("the suitcase") to the ground suppression resources. The Firewatch Bell 209 is considered a type 2 aircraft for helispot sizing purposes.

(2) **Logistical**

    (a)   Live video downlink

    (b)   Infrared imagery/video

    (c)   Mapping

When in the Logistical Profile, the Firewatch Platform will initially request entry into the Fire Traffic Area at altitude, 1000 feet or more above the Aerial Supervision Platform. Entry into the FTA at this altitude allows the Firewatch Platform to get the "big picture" of the incident for the live video feed mission, initial infrared imagery work and video work, and orientation to the incident and aircraft working the incident.

If mapping the incident is part of the mission, the Firewatch Platform will request transition to 500 feet agl and below to complete the mission. The Firewatch ATGS will give the Aerial Supervision Platform an initial map starting point and either a clockwise or counterclockwise rotation of the perimeter request.

Chapter 6 – Suppression Chemicals

Wildland fire suppressants and retardants are chemical agents applied to burning and adjacent fuels. Only chemicals that are on the Qualified Products List (QPL) shall be used, and only for the delivery method approved. See the Forest Service's wildland fire chemicals Web site for details: http://www.fs.fed.us/rm/fire/wfcs/index.htm

Refer to *the Interagency Standards for Fire and Fire Aviation Operations* or the Web site noted above for the most current information on fire chemicals and their use.

1) Definitions

a) **Suppressants (Direct Attack only):** – A fire suppression chemical applied directly to the flame base to extinguish the flame (water, foam, gel/water enhancer).

- **Foam fire suppressants** contain foaming and/or wetting agents. The foaming agents and percentage concentrate added affect the accuracy of an aerial drop, how fast the water drains from the foam, and how well the product clings to the fuel surfaces. The wetting agents increase the ability of the drained water to penetrate fuels. These products are dependent on the water they contain to suppress the fire. Once the water they contain has evaporated, they are no longer effective. Foam may be applied by engines, portable pumps, helicopters, and SEATs. Some agencies also allow application of foam from fixed-wing water scoopers.

  - **Wet Water** foam concentrates mixed at 0.1 - 0.3 percent will produce a wet water solution (low foam, high wetting ability).

- **Water enhancers** contain ingredients designed to alter the physical characteristics of water to increase viscosity, accuracy of the drop, or adhesion to fuels. They improve the ability of water to cling to vertical and smooth surfaces. The consistency of these products can change depending on the quality of the water used for mixing. Once the water they contain has evaporated, they are no longer effective. They are fully approved for use in helicopter buckets and engine application. Many are also approved, at specific mix ratios, for use in SEATs, and fixed tank helicopters.

b) **Long-Term Retardant (Direct and Indirect Attack):**

Long-term retardants contain fertilizer salts that change the way fuels burn. They are effective even after the water has evaporated, hence the name, "long-term". Retardants may be applied by large airtankers, single engine airtankers (SEATs) helicopter buckets, and ground engines. Some retardant products are approved for fixed tank helicopters. See the QPL for specific uses for each product.

Recommended coverage levels and guidelines for use can be found in the 10 Principles of Retardant Application, NFES 2048, PMS 440-2 pocket card. Retardant mixing, blending, testing, and sampling requirements can be found at the WFCS Web site, Lot Acceptance and Quality Assurance page: http://www.fs.fed.us/rm/fire/wfcs/laqa.htm.

In general, one can expect chemicals to remain effective for the following amounts of time:

- Long-Term Retardants – Days to Weeks (or until removed by environmental elements such as rain or wind)

- Foams – Minutes

- Water Enhancers/Gels - Minutes up to possibly an hour or more (direct sunlight breaks down gels faster). Time will vary according to weather conditions (heat, humidity, wind, etc.)

2) Approved Fire Chemicals

Many different long term retardants, foams and water enhancers are approved for use. Prior to approval these agents must meet rigid criteria to ensure that they are environmentally safe, effective as a retardant or suppressant, and that the chemicals do not harm aircraft surfaces. Chemical concentrates may be dry powder or liquid concentrates prior to mixing, depending on manufacture. All USDA/USDI bases must use chemicals that are either fully approved or "conditionally approved" during field evaluations for full approval.

3) Retardant Mixing Facilities

Long-term retardants are available from a variety of facilities including fire incident locations. Tactical effectiveness and cost effectiveness are greatly enhanced when temporary portable mix facilities are set up on or near the incident. Facilities may be ordered through the incident management system, from agency fire caches or directly from retardant manufacturers. Long-term retardants are available or can be mixed from:

a) Permanent or Reload Retardant Bases

b) Remote Retardant Base: Modular retardant base entirely transportable by Type 1 helicopter, which are excellent for remote areas with no road access.

c) Portable Retardant Base: Totally portable retardant mixing system used primarily to mix and load retardant into airtankers (SEATs, large airtankers and VLATs), helicopters and ground units.

d) Portable Helicopter Retardant System: Similar to the Portable Retardant Base but is more specifically designed for use by helicopters.

4) Airtanker Base Information

Information regarding the management and operation of airtanker bases and information about specific airtanker bases can be found in the following documents:

a) *Interagency Airtanker Base Operations Guide*, PMS 507: This guide defines and standardizes interagency operating procedures at all airtanker bases for contractor and government employees.

b) *Interagency Airtanker Base Directory* – The directory is intended to aid wildland fire managers, pilots, and contractors who operate at airtanker bases (Reference NFES 2537).

c) *Wildland Fire Chemicals Web site*: found at http://www.fs.fed.us/rm/fire/wfcs/index.htm

5) Aerial Fire Chemical Application Safety

a) Personnel and equipment in the flight path of intended aerial drops should move to a location that will decrease the possibility of being hit with a drop.

b) Personnel near aerial drops should be alert for objects (tree limbs, rocks, etc.) that the drop could dislodge. The Incident Response Pocket Guide (IRPG) provides additional safety information for personnel in drop areas.

c) During training or briefings, inform all fire personnel of environmental guidelines and requirements for fire chemicals application and avoid contact with waterways.

d) Avoid dipping from rivers or lakes with a helicopter bucket containing residual fire chemicals without first cleaning/washing down the bucket.

e) Avoid scooping from rivers or lakes with fixed-wing aircraft or helicopter buckets containing residual fire chemicals without first cleaning the tank, aircraft underbody or bucket.

f) Consider setting up an adjacent reload site and manage the fire chemicals in portable tanks or terminate the use of chemicals for that application.

g) Some fire chemicals may be irritating to skin. Wash exposed areas as soon as possible after contact.

6) Environmental and Wilderness Effects

Retardant use in wilderness can be inconsistent with the requirement to protect and preserve natural conditions. It may be allowed if it is the minimum necessary tactic to accomplish fire and wilderness management objectives. Retardant drops should be planned to minimize effects on natural resources and future recreation use of the area. "Fugitive" colored retardant is designed to fade over time and may be a recommended tool in sensitive areas.

7) Waterway and Avoidance Area Policy

Interagency Policy for Aerial and Ground Delivery of Wildland Fire Chemicals Near Waterways and Other Avoidance Areas

This policy has been adopted from the 2000 and 2009 updated Guidelines for Aerial Delivery of all wildland fire chemicals, including retardant, foam and water enhancers which were established and approved by the Forest Service (FS) and the Department of the Interior (DOI). It has been expanded to include additional avoidance areas for aerial delivery of fire chemicals as designated by individual agencies and includes additional FS reporting requirements.

*This policy **does not** require the helicopter or airtanker pilot-in-command to fly in such a way as to endanger his or her aircraft, other aircraft, or structures or compromise ground personnel safety.*

Aerial Delivery Policy	Ground Delivery Policy
• Avoid aerial application of all wildland fire chemicals within 300 feet (ft.) of waterways. • Additional mapped avoidance areas may be designated by individual agency. • For FS, whenever practical, as determined by the fire incident commander, use water or other less toxic wildland fire chemical suppressants for direct attack or less toxic approved fire retardants in areas occupied by threatened, endangered, proposed, candidate or sensitive species (TEPCS) or their designated critical habitats.	• Avoid application of all wildland fire chemicals into waterways or mapped avoidance areas.

Definition of Waterway:

> Any body of water (including lakes, rivers, streams and ponds) whether or not it contains aquatic life.

Definition of Waterway Buffer:

> 300 ft. distance on either side of a waterway.

Definition of Additional Mapped Avoidance Areas:

> Other areas requiring additional protection outside of the 300 ft. waterway buffer. For FS, this may include certain dry intermittent or ephemeral streams for resource protection.

Guidance for pilots:

Pilots will avoid all waterways and additional mapped avoidance areas designated by individual agencies.

To meet the 300 ft waterway buffer zone or additional mapped avoidance areas guideline, implement the following:

• **All Aircraft**: When approaching a waterway or riparian vegetation visible to the pilot (to assist in identification if waterways) or other avoidance areas, the pilot shall terminate application of wildland fire chemical approximately 300 ft before reaching the area. When flying over a waterway, the pilot shall not begin application of wildland fire chemical until 300 ft. after crossing the far bank or shore. The pilot shall make adjustments for airspeed and ambient conditions such as wind to avoid the application of wildland fire chemicals within the 300 ft. buffer zone.

Additional guidance to pilots for any aircraft supporting a fire on FS lands:

- FS may have additional mapped avoidance areas for TEPCS species, waterway buffers exceeding 300 ft. or certain intermittent or ephemeral waterways that are identified as avoidance areas for resource protection. Any aerial supervision resource should inquire if these avoidance areas exist on any FS fire they are providing support to.

- Prior to fire retardant application, all aerial supervision and/or pilots shall be briefed by dispatch on the locations of all TEPCS or other avoidance areas in the vicinity.

- If operationally feasible, pilots or the aerial supervision shall make a 'dry run' over the intended application area to identify avoidance areas and waterways in the vicinity of the wildland fire.

- Pilots should be provided avoidance area maps and information at all briefings (if not dispatched from one geographic area/unit and delivering to another geographic area).

Exceptions for USDA Forest Service:

- Deviations from the policy are allowed only for the protection of life or safety (public and firefighter).

Exceptions for all other Agencies:

- When alternative line construction tactics are not available due to terrain constraints, congested area, life and property concerns or lack of ground personnel, it is acceptable to anchor the wildland fire chemical application to the waterway. When anchoring a wildland fire chemical line to a waterway, use the most accurate method of delivery in order to minimize placement of wildland fire chemical in the waterway (e.g., a helicopter rather than a heavy airtanker).

- Deviations from the policy are acceptable when life or property is threatened and the use of wildland fire chemical can be reasonably expected to alleviate the threat.

- When potential damage to natural resources outweighs possible loss of aquatic life, the unit administrator may approve a deviation from these guidelines.

Reporting Requirements of Aerially Delivered Wildland Fire Chemicals into Waterways, Waterway buffer areas and Mapped Avoidance Areas

During training or briefings, inform field personnel of:

- environmental guidelines for fire chemical application,

- requirements for avoiding contact with waterways,

- additional mapped avoidance areas as designated by individual agency, and

- their responsibility for upward reporting in the event of application, for whatever reason, into avoidance areas.

If application of wildland fire chemical occurs or anyone believes it may have been introduced within waterway, waterway buffered areas or other mapped avoidance areas, the following is required as appropriate:

- they should inform their supervisor,

- the information will be forwarded to incident management and the agency administrator, usually through the resource advisor,

- the incident or host authorities must immediately contact specialists within the local jurisdiction, and

- notifications and reporting will be completed as soon as possible.

Procedures have been implemented for the required reporting. All information, including reporting tools and instructions are posted on the FS wildland fire chemicals Web site at: http://www.fs.fed.us/rm/fire/wfcs and fire retardant site at: http://www.fs.fed.us/fire/retardant/. The FS has additional reporting requirements for threatened, endangered, proposed, candidate and FS listed sensitive species for aerially delivered fire retardant only. This requirement resulted from the Forest Service's acceptance of Biological Opinions received from the National Marine Fisheries Service (NMFS) and the Fish and Wildlife Service (FWS) and the 2011 Record of Decision for Nationwide Aerial Application of Fire Retardant on National Forest System Lands. The procedures, reporting tools and instructions can be found at the same website listed above.

Endangered Species Act, (ESA) Emergency consultation

The FS has completed consultation with regulatory agencies (FWS and NOAA) for aerial delivery of fire retardant (only) on National Forest System lands; please refer to the FS fire retardant site at http://www.fs.fed.us/fire/retardant/ for additional information and re-initiation of consultation requirements.

The following provisions are guidance for complying with the emergency section 7 consultation procedures of the ESA for wildland fire chemicals. These provisions do not alter or diminish an action agency's responsibilities under the ESA.

Where T&E species or their habitats are potentially affected by application of wildland fire chemicals, the following additional procedures apply and shall be documented in initial or subsequent fire reports.

- As soon as practicable after application of wildland fire chemical near waterways or other avoidance area as designated by agency, determine whether the application has caused any adverse effects to a T&E species or their habitat. This can be accomplished by the following:

- Ground application of wildland fire chemical outside a waterway is presumed to avoid adverse effects to aquatic species and no further consultation for aquatic species is necessary.

- Aerial application of wildland fire chemical outside 300 ft. of a waterway is presumed to avoid adverse effects to aquatic species and no further consultation for aquatic species is necessary.

- Aerial application of wildland fire chemical within 300 ft. of a waterway requires that the unit administrator determine whether there have been any adverse effects to T&E species within the waterway. If no adverse effects to aquatic T&E species or their habitats, no additional requirement to consult on aquatic species with FWS or NMFS is required.

- Application of wildland fire chemical within other avoidance areas as designated by agency requires the agency administrator to determine whether there have been any adverse effects to T&E species. If there are no adverse effects to species or their habitats there is no additional requirement to consult with FWS or NMFS

If the action agency determines that there were adverse effects on T&E species or their habitats then the action agency must consult with FWS and NMFS, as required by 50 CFR 402.05 (Emergencies). Procedures for emergency consultation are described in the *Interagency Consultation Handbook*, Chapter 8 (March, 1998). In the case of a long duration incident, emergency consultation should be initiated as soon as practical during the event. Otherwise, post-event consultation is appropriate. The initiation of the consultation is the responsibility of the unit administrator.

This page intentionally left blank.

Chapter 7- Aerial Supervision Mission Procedures

Aerial Supervision operations are conducted in demanding flight conditions in a high workload/multi-tasking environment. Because of this, standardization of procedures is important to enhance safety, effectiveness, efficiency, and professionalism. This chapter addresses common procedures to be observed by all aerial supervision specialists as well as unique guidance for Lead, ATCO, ASM, ATGS, and HLCO personnel.

The actions listed below pertain to all modes of aerial supervision (Lead, ATCO, ASM, ATGS, and HLCO). Methods for performing these actions differ between disciplines and are often refined as flight crew relationships develop.

Aerial Supervision Procedures

1) Pre-Mission Procedures

a) **Pilot Qualification Card & Aircraft Data Card** – Review these cards and verify the pilot and aircraft are authorized for air tactical missions.

b) **Flight & Duty Limitations** – Determine when pilot's duty day began and if sufficient flight/duty time is remaining. If not, order a relief pilot.

c) **Aircraft Maintenance** – Verify aircraft has sufficient time remaining before next scheduled maintenance. If not, order another aircraft.

d) **Aircraft Preparation** – Both the pilot and ATGS have responsibilities.

    i) **Pilot Preflight Responsibilities** – Include but not limited to:

        (1) Aircraft preflight inspection.

        (2) Calculate weight and balance of passengers and equipment.

        (3) Fueling: Discuss fuel requirements and limitations for mission with ATGS. Ensure proper fueling.

        (4) Possess/wear approved personal protective equipment.

        (5) File a flight plan as needed.

        (6) Obtain a weather briefing.

    ii) **Aerial Supervisor Preflight Responsibilities**

        (1) Inspect communications system. Install NIFC radio package if required.

        (2) Program VHF-FM tactical frequencies in radio (coordinate with pilot).

        (3) Perform a radio check.

        (4) Load air tactical equipment.

        (5) Assist pilot as requested with crew duties.

e) **Procurement Agreements** – The aerial supervisor should be familiar with the basic terms of the procurement agreement/contract.

f) **Obtain a Mission Briefing** – Whether the air tactical mission is initial attack or a project incident, all types of aerial supervision personnel must obtain pertinent incident information. Dispatch centers must provide an **Aircraft Dispatch Form**.

    i) **Initial Attack Briefings** – The following information can be recorded on a mission record or similar form.

        (1) Incident name or number

        (2) Agency responsible

        (3) Incident location – legal location, latitude/longitude and VOR

        (4) Frequencies and tones: Double check operating mode (N,W,D) and tones.

        (5) Flight following

        (6) Air-to-Ground

        (7) Air-to-Air (FM and/or AM)

        (8) Contacts: ground and air

        (9) Air resources assigned or to be assigned, ETEs, type, and identifier

        (10) Other resources dispatched (as practical)

        (11) Approximate incident size and fire behavior

        (12) Other available air resources

        (13) Aerial and ground **hazards**

        (14) Special information such as land status, watershed, wilderness, and urban interface.

        (15) Airtanker reload base options and turnaround times.

    ii) **Extended Attack Briefings** – If possible, aerial supervision personnel should attend incident briefings. If this is not possible critical information should be relayed by phone, radio, fax or messenger. A copy of the IAP is essential. Aerial supervision personnel may have to seek some of this information:

        (1) Incident objectives by division

        (2) Organization Assignment List (ICS 203) or list of key operations people

        (3) Air Operations Summary (ICS 220) or list of assigned aircraft

        (4) List of all aircraft by make/model and identification

          (5)   Incident Radio Communication Plan (ICS 205) or list of frequencies

          (6)   Incident Map

          (7)   Fire Behavior Report and local weather

          (8)   Air resource availability/status

          (9)   Incident Medevac Plan and Medevac helicopter assigned

g) **Mission Safety Briefing for Pilot** – Prior to departure on an air tactical mission the aerial supervisor will brief the pilot on the following.

    i)   General scope of the mission

    ii)   Incident location: latitude-longitude and bearing-distance

    iii)   Resources assigned

    iv)   Radio frequencies

    v)   Special information including hazards and military operations

    vi)   Expected duration of mission

h) **Pre Takeoff Responsibilities**

    i)   Pilot responsibilities

        (1)   Complete the appropriate aircraft checklists.

        (2)   Complete pre-flight including passenger safety briefing.

        (3)   Confirm fuel supply.

        (4)   Obtain route clearances through Special Use Airspace as required.

        (5)   Program GPS to incident location.

    ii)   ATGS/ATS responsibilities

        (1)   Obtain, record, and set local altimeter setting (from pilot or airport advisory).

        (2)   Program radios (AM/FM) – Check with pilot before programming the AM.

        (3)   Confirm fuel supply and flight time available for mission.

        (4)   Check with dispatch regarding status of military aviation operations (Restricted, MOA's, MTR's) and Temporary Flight Restrictions.

        (5)   Perform start, taxi, and pre-takeoff checklists.

2) Enroute Procedures

a) **After Take Off**

    i)   Record take off time (takeoff roll).

    ii)   Observe sterile cockpit protocol as previously agreed to with pilot.

iii) Establish Flight Following:

(1) Identify yourself: (ex: "Boise Dispatch Air Attack 1SA on National Flight Following".)

(2) Give required flight following information: (ex: "Air Attack 1SA is off Boise enroute to the Dry Fire, 2 souls on board, 4 hours fuel, ETE 15 Minutes".)

(3) Confirm AFF.

iv) Notify pilot of any information or situation affecting the flight (ATGS/ATS).

v) Assist pilot as requested. Be a proactive crewmember (ATGS/ATS).

vi) Complete mission checklist.

b) **Enroute Communications** – Maintain communications with dispatch and other aircraft concerning:

i) Incident air resource updates.

ii) Status of special use airspace (TFR, restricted, etc.).

iii) Coordination with responding air resources can be done on the assigned Air-to-Air frequency provided it does not interfere with operations over the incident.

iv) **Monitor the fire frequencies to enhance situational awareness when you arrive on scene.**

3) Airspace Coordination Procedures

Safety, effectiveness, and efficiency are often established in the first minutes of the mission. These procedures are standard for all firefighting aircraft.

a) **FTA Entry**– 12 nautical miles from the center point of the incident, aerial supervision personnel **must** follow the procedures listed below. There are three scenarios; Aerial supervision is on scene, aerial supervision is not on scene, but other aircraft are, or there are no aircraft on scene.

Scenario 1: Aerial Supervision is on scene:

i) Notify the dispatch center of your position.

ii) Change to incident frequencies.

iii) Give 12-mile radio call to aerial supervision. Give your location and altitude.

iv) Obtain clearance into FTA by getting:

(1) Altimeter setting

(2) FTA Entry Altitude

(3) Altitude of aerial supervision

(4) Altitudes of other aircraft

(5) Enter the incident airspace, as briefed.

(6) Watch for other aircraft and call out a distance and clock reference when you spot the on scene aerial supervision.

(7) Receive transition briefing and confirm positive handoff of aerial supervision responsibilities.

(8) (8) Outgoing aerial supervision will notify dispatch and incoming aerial supervision will notify IC/ground personnel and confirm objectives and priorities.

Scenario 2: Aerial supervision is not on scene, but other aircraft are:

i) Notify dispatch of your position.

ii) Change to incident frequencies.

iii) Give 12-mile blind radio call on Victor (AM). Give your location, altitude, and intentions. An on scene aircraft should respond on Victor.

iv) Obtain clearance into FTA by getting:

(1) Altimeter setting

(2) FTA Entry Altitude

(3) Altitudes and locations of other aircraft on scene

(4) Enter the incident airspace, as briefed with on scene aircraft.

(5) Watch for other aircraft and call out a distance and clock reference when you spot the on scene aircraft.

(6) Get status of all on scene aircraft (location, mission type, etc.)

(7) Call IC and get objectives and priorities.

(8) Notify dispatch you on scene and now the incident aerial supervision.

Scenario 3: There are no aircraft on scene:

i) Give 12-mile blind radio call to aerial supervision on Victor (AM). Give your location, altitude, and intentions.

ii) Call the IC/ground personnel on the assigned FM air-to-ground frequency and verify no other aircraft are on scene.

iii) Proceed to the incident. Stay at least 2,500' AGL and watch for other aircraft.

iv) Get center point and record size up information.

v) Call dispatch, notify you are the on scene aerial supervision and provide size up.

vi) Call the IC/ground forces and establish objectives and priorities.

b) **Entering Incident Airspace** - ATGS fixed wing enter the airspace in a right hand pattern at 2,500 feet AGL unless the situation dictates a different altitude (smoke/terrain), Leadplane enter in a left pattern, and ASM or HLCO enter in either depending on the situation.

c) **Arrival on Scene**

    i) Initial Responsibilities – Aerial supervision personnel **must**:

        (1) Watch for aircraft and make visual/verbal contact with each one.

        (2) Determine ground elevation to establish FTA altitudes for incoming aircraft including helicopters, airtankers, lead/ASM, smokejumpers, relief aerial supervision, and media ("the stack").

        (3) Determine flight hazards – Power lines, antennas, snags, terrain, thunder storm activity, excessive wind, poor visibility, airspace conflicts, etc.

        (4) Confirm incident objectives and priorities with the IC/ground personnel.

d) **Incoming Aircraft** – All aircraft will receive a briefing and clearance into the FTA. Briefings typically occur in three phases: initial, tactical, and departure.

    i) **Initial Briefing** – When aircraft check in at the 12 mile ring, **give** the following:

        (1) Altimeter setting

        (2) Altitude they are cleared in at.

            (a) Give airtankers and other fixed wing aircraft a hard altitude.

            (b) Give helicopters a hard ceiling.

            (c) Give media a hard floor.

        (3) Your altitude.

        (4) Altitudes and locations of other aircraft on scene.

        (5) General area of the fire to head for.

        (6) For airtankers: Give portion of load and coverage level. For helicopters: Give ground contact and mission type.

        (7) Hazards – Describe general hazards (weather, turbulence, visibility, towers/power lines, etc.).

    ii) **Tactical briefing** – This briefing occurs when the incoming aircraft has the drop/mission area in sight.

        (1) **Objective** – Describe the objective or intent of the drop/mission.

        (2) **Target description** –Start with a large geographic area and work it down to the specific point(s).

(3) **Ground contacts and frequencies** - Helicopter pilots need the A/G frequency and a ground contact.

(4) **Hazards** – Identify specific hazards that may be encountered in the drop/mission area.

(5) **Drop clearance** – Establish the line or mission area is clear and notify tanker/helicopter pilot they are clear to drop/perform their mission.

iii) **Departure briefing**

(1) **Drop/mission evaluation** –Assess the drop/mission effectiveness and notify airtanker/helicopter pilot. For airtankers, use terms such as early or late, right or left, and high or low. Helicopter feedback is mission specific.

(2) **Reload Instructions** – For airtankers, they need reload instructions and a location. Always confirm reload instructions with the IC/ground personnel. Work directly with ground personnel to determine helicopter needs.

(3) **Dispatch** – Notify dispatch of reload instructions (load and return, hold, released, etc).

e) **More on Target Description** – Direct aviation resources to mission areas and targets. Concise messages using standard terminology expedite the task and increase safety.

i) Target Description – A standard target description includes the following:

(1) Target location

(2) Drop objectives (intent of drop)

(3) Type of drop/coverage level

(4) Hazards

(5) Clearance to drop

Methods to describe targets:

(a) GPS reference points – in limited visibility (inversions), lat & long references can significantly increase safety while reducing radio traffic.

Note: Be aware that the standard datum and coordinate format aviation GPS equipment is WGS 84 and decimal minutes whereas many GPS units used by ground personnel default to a NAD 27 datum and a degrees, minutes, seconds format. The use of different datums and formats may result in misinterpreting the location of a specific target. Ensure that the target location is confirmed with ground personnel.

  (b) Fire anatomy: Left and right flank, head, heel (tail in AK), etc.

  (c) Geographic features: Ridges, saddles, spur ridges, lakes, streams, etc.

  (d) Cardinal directions: Specify true or magnetic. Be exact! Often directions are generalized and create confusion.

  (e) Specific activity: Dozer working, firing operation, parked vehicles, previous drop, etc.

  (f) Elevation: Specify above sea level (MSL) or above ground level (AGL).

  (g) Incident features: Helibase, helispots, fireline, and division breaks, etc.

  (h) Standard terminology: Standard terms are in the glossary.

 (6) **Guiding Aircraft**

  (a) Clock directions, left or right, etc.

  (b) Signal mirrors, ground panels, lights, etc.

  (c) Have an on scene aircraft lead new aircraft to the target area.

  (d) Discuss target locations the when other aircraft is in a good position to see it.

f) **Air Traffic Coordination** – Terrain, visibility, number and type of aircraft, and TFR dimensions, and other factors influence requirements for maintaining safe separation.

General Air Traffic Coordination Principles

i) **Pilots maintain aircraft separation by**:

 (1) Using standard aviation 'see and avoid' visual flight rules

 (2) Having access to the appropriate air-to-air frequency for position reporting

 (3) Adhering to Fire Traffic Area (FTA) procedures

ii) **Aerial Supervisors Ensure Aircraft Separation by**:

 (1) Structuring the incident airspace and briefing pilots

 (2) Monitoring radio communications for:

 (3) Pilot-to-pilot position reports

 (4) Blind call position reports

 (5) Visually tracking aircraft as needed

 (6) Giving specific directions to pilots as needed

 (7) Advising pilots on the location and heading of other aircraft

Note: The coordinates of the incident must be verified, updated as needed, and communicated to Dispatch to ensure that inbound incident aircraft can determine the appropriate points at which to initiate initial contact and/or hold if communications with controlling aircraft are not established.

iii) **Vertical Separation**

    (1)   500 feet is the minimum vertical separation for missions in the same airspace. **1,000 feet is preferred and should be used whenever possible.**

    (2)   Assigning block altitudes (with vertical range up to 500 feet) to orbiting fixed-wing is preferred in windy or active thermal conditions.

    (3)   Vertical stacking airtankers is discouraged. Utilize a racetrack pattern if multiple airtankers are on scene.

    (4)   It's common practice to put media helicopters above the ATGS in order to keep them away from firefighting aircraft.

    (5)   Standard operational altitudes and patterns are:

Table 8. Standard Operational Altitudes and Patterns		
Mission	**AGL (feet)**	**Normal Pattern**
Media	As assigned	Right or left
ATGS – Fixed Wing	2000 to 2500	Right
ATGS – Helicopter	500 to 2000	Right or left
Airtanker Orbit	1000 to 1500	Left – outside to observe
Airtanker Maneuvering	150 to 1000	Left
Leadplane	150 to 1000	Left
Helicopters	0 to 500	Left or right
Smokejumper Ram Air Chute	3000	Left
Smokejumper Round Chute	1500	Left
Paracargo	150 to 1500	Left

iv) **Horizontal Separation**

    (1)   Visibility must be good enough for other aircraft to see each other and maintain separation.

    (2)   Flight patterns must be adequate, i.e. not hindered by terrain.

        (a)   Consult pilots before finalizing patterns and routes.

        (b)   Advise pilots on location of other aircraft if visual contact has not been reported.

        (c)   Air to air frequency must be accessible for pilots to give position reports.

(d)   Geographic references, such as a ridges or a river, can be used to separate aircraft provided aircraft maintain assigned flight patterns.

(e)   No fly zones must be established to ensure safe separation when simultaneous missions at the same elevation are within close proximity.

(f)   Below ridges: For operations separated by a ridge, a "no-fly zone" 500 feet vertically below the ridge top can be established to ensure separation.

(g)   Near geographic dividing lines: If simultaneous operations near the dividing line are in conflict, a horizontal "no-fly zone" must be established or missions must be sequenced to ensure adequate separation.

v)   **Incident Entry and Exit Corridors** – Aerial supervision shall determine incident entry/exit corridors as needed. All aircraft must be notified of corridors. If an entry corridor and exit corridor cannot be separated horizontally, then they must be separated vertically (refer to Incident Ingress/Egress discussion above).

vi)   **Holding Areas and Initial Points** – The aerial supervisor assigns incoming aircraft to non-conflicting airspaces, or holding areas, as needed. Coordinates or a geographic reference work best

(1)   **Airtankers** can be held near an incident, two or three at a time, in the same holding area. More than one holding area may be used. Considerations include:

(a)   Pilots must be aware of other aircraft in the holding area.

(b)   Pilots must be able to communicate position reports to each other

(c)   Holding area must be clearly defined – by a geographic reference point or distance and direction relative to the incident. Usually a "race track" pattern with one tanker following the other at the same altitude providing their own visual separation.

(2)   **Helicopters** can be held on the ground or in the air as needed to maintain adequate separation. Considerations include:

(a)   Common helicopter holding areas include obvious landmarks, helispots, helibase, dipsites, etc. Any of these locations may be utilized as a virtual fence.

(b)   Pilots should be able to maintain forward flight rather than constant hover.

(c)   Long periods of holding helicopters should be done on the ground.

vii) **Sequencing** – Aircraft may be sequenced into the same area provided each aircraft can complete its mission and exit the area before the next aircraft enters the area. Sequencing requires close supervision. **Caution:** Consider wake turbulence when sequencing any type of aircraft.

    (1) **Sequencing Airtankers and Helicopters** – Helicopters can be held at a safe distance from drop site until an airtanker has completed its drop.

    (2) **Sequencing Airtankers and Paracargo** – Stage aircraft 180^0 apart in the same flight pattern so flights over the target area are controlled by position in orbit.

viii) **Interval Dispatching** – To reduce the problem of too many airtankers over an incident at the same time, ask dispatch or the ATB to launch airtankers at intervals (usually 10 to 15 minutes).

ix) **Checkpoints and Virtual Fences** – Effective for maintaining air traffic control with minimal radio traffic on the Air-to-Air frequency. Pilots are instructed to report their location and destination "in the blind" when crossing check points. Pilots may be required to report arrival at a virtual fence and wait for clearance from ATGS before proceeding. Know geographic locations make effective check points and virtual fences.

    (1) **Fixed Wing Checkpoints** – Orbit location (turning base, on downwind, on final), crossing highway, over mountain, etc.

    (2) **Helicopter Checkpoints** – Departures from helispots or dipsites, arrival at target or helispots, etc.

    (3) **Virtual Fences** – Roads, power lines, ridges, lakes, etc.

x) **Helicopter routes**: Established for repetitive missions from helibase to helispots or sling points, from dipsites to targets, etc. For safety, efficiency and monitoring, the ATGS, in consultation with the helibase manager and/or helicopter pilots, will ensure flight routes and communications procedures have been established and are known:

    (1) **Well Defined Routes** – Up one stream and down another, up one side of drainage and down the other side, up one side of a spur ridge and down the other, etc.

    (2) **Air to Air Communications** – Pilots must have ready access to the Air-to-Air frequency in order to maintain separation. If needed, separate Air-to-Air frequencies should be established for helicopters and airtankers. The original air to air frequency should be retained for airtankers.

    (3) **Checkpoints** – Determine as needed for blind calls.

xi) **Helicopter Daisy Chains** – Two or more helicopters can be assigned to the same targets and dipsites for repeated water drops. The ATGS, in consultation with helicopter pilots, will establish a "daisy-chain" flight route for these operations.

xii) **Helicopter Recon Flights** – These flights can be difficult to monitor. Consider the following procedures to maintain safe separation of aircraft:

(1) Schedule recon flights during slow periods, i.e., when airtankers are loading.

(2) Assign a specific route for the recon, ex. clockwise around and 100 yards outside the incident perimeter.

(3) Establish Check Points, i.e. division breaks, helispots, drainages, etc.

xiii) **Intersecting Routes** – Intersecting aircraft routes shall be clearly identifiable geographically. Intersections shall have a minimum of 500 feet vertical separation.

xiv) **Non Standard Patterns** – Occasionally terrain, visibility, wind direction or other factors require flight patterns are modified or reversed. The mission pilot, LEAD, or HLCO shall advise ATGS of situation and request a deviation from standard procedures. The ATGS will advise other aircraft before granting the request.

g) **Coordination Between Types of Aerial Supervisors** – Each incident is unique and circumstances dictate that workload sharing between Lead, ATGS, HLCO and ASM as their responsibilities overlap in several areas. By prior agreement and after receiving a good briefing, a positive working relationship can be established.

It is important that ATGS, ASM, Lead, and HLCO work as a team and share workload commensurate with fire complexity, training and position authority.

i) **Airtanker Mission Sequence between ATGS and Lead/ASM**

(1) ATGS and ground operations jointly determine tactical objectives.

(2) ATGS briefs Lead/ASM on next target, coverage level, etc.

(3) Airtanker makes 12 mile check-in with ATGS or Lead.

(4) If the airtanker checks in with ATGS, ATGS will brief airtanker or pass on to Lead/ASM (preferred).

(5) Lead/ASM briefs airtanker on target, coverage level, etc.

(6) ATGS clears conflicting air resources from the airspace and gives verbal clearance to Lead/ASM for low level operations. The ATGS may also elect to hand off conflicting air resources to Lead/ASM in order to reduce radio traffic.

(7) ATGS clears ground personnel from target area

(8) ATGS will maintain radio silence on Air-to-Air while Lead/ASM and airtanker are working, particularly when on final approach or

exiting the drop area unless the drop needs to be called off. If incoming airtankers reporting 12 miles out and are in conflict with ongoing operations, than a separate airtanker briefing frequency for the Leadplane and airtanker in tow should be established. This can be VHF-AM or FM.

(9) Lead/ASM will do low level recon to determine hazards, targets, elevations, location of people, equipment, facilities, safe patterns and exit routes, etc.

(10) Lead/ASM briefs airtanker on objectives, flight route, coverage level, drift potential and hazards.

(11) Lead/ASM may make a dry run with airtanker on the intended target.

(12) ATGS confirms ground personnel are clear of target area

(13) Airtanker makes drop(s). Airtanker may or may not require a lead.

(14) ATGS pilot positions aircraft to monitor and evaluate drop

(15) ATGS evaluates drop and gets ground feedback. Leadplane may also be able to evaluate drop. Evaluation includes accuracy, coverage level, coverage uniformity, etc. Evaluation may reveal need to adjust to left or right. These adjustments are expressed in wing-spans or rotor-spans, not feet or yards.

(16) ATGS gives feedback to Leadplane and airtanker pilot after clear of drop area (Leadplane and airtanker may have already heard same feedback from ground).

(17) Lead/ASM and airtanker make adjustments as needed on subsequent drops.

(18) Lead/ASM gives airtanker reload instructions based on instruction from ATGS.

(19) ATGS informs ground when clear to return to work area.

(20) Airtanker informs dispatch on status – load and return or hold.

h) **Assuming ATCO Duties** – When a Lead/ASM is unavailable due to days off, arrival delays, out of flight hours, or refueling, the ATGS will assume the ATCO. The ATGS must maintain a minimum altitude of 500 ft AGL performing ATCO duties.

i) **Maintaining Air Tactics Continuity** – Complex air operations or air operations involving a mix of air resources requires continuous supervision by an ATGS, ASM, Lead, or HLCO. To maintain continuous supervision, the following procedures should be followed. Good planning will ensure continuity:

i) Use ASM to fill gaps in ATGS coverage and manage air/ground operations in designated areas on complex incidents.

ii)   Stagger aircraft refueling so all aircraft are not down simultaneously.

iii)   Stagger airtankers to maintain continuous coverage.

iv)   Monitor flight times. Anticipate the need for a relief pilot, Leadplane or other air resource. Notify dispatcher or AOBD in a timely manner.

v)   Anticipate fuel needs and facilitate obtaining fueling facilities near the incident.

vi)   Recommend activation of portable reload bases to reduce turn-around time.

vii)   Coordinate refuel and relief needs between aerial supervisors to ensure continuity of airspace management/supervision.

j) **Relief Guidelines** – Aerial supervision is mentally demanding. Long flight hours result in mental fatigue, reduced effectiveness, and compromised safety. Consider the following staffing guidelines:

i)   If the aerial supervisor will fly more than 4 hours on any one flight, order a relief.

ii)   On multi-day incidents, assign a second aerial supervisor and rotate about every 3 hours.

k) **Diversion of Aerial Resources** –Higher priority incidents require diversion of air resources. A reassignment may be given through dispatch or through IC/Operations. Aerial supervision may also be diverted to manage the new incident. Upon receiving a divert notice, the aerial supervisor must release and brief the requested resources on the following:

i)   Incident location

ii)   Air and ground contacts

iii)   Radio frequencies

Note: Tactical aviation resources may be diverted to a higher priority incident. The aerial supervisor should be advised by dispatch and modify incident tactics.

No Divert Request – Under the following situations, the IC can request through dispatch that no airtanker be diverted to other incidents when an imminent threat to life of a firefighter or civilian exists.

4) Coordination with Ground Personnel

On type I & II incidents, aerial supervisors work with Air Operations, Operations, Division Supervisors, and other line personnel. On type III & IV incidents, aerial supervisors work primarily with the IC, ground crews, and dispatch. Aerial supervisors provide intelligence to tactical personnel and dispatchers in order to facilitate the dissemination of valid information provided during the briefing process.

a) **Provide Fire Information and Size up for Tactical Planning**

b) **Size up the Fire** – Make initial assessment and communicate critical safety, strategy, and tactics inputs to ground contact and/or dispatch. **Get oriented** – Develop a mental or **sketched map** of the incident that includes:

    i) Cardinal directions

    ii) Landmarks: Roads, streams, lakes, mountains, improvements, etc.

    iii) Fire flanks, head, etc.

    iv) Visible work accomplished: Dozer lines, handline, retardant line, etc.

    v) Record GPS coordinates to identify reference points.

    vi) Review IAP map; note frequencies, aircraft assignments/availability, division breaks, helispots, etc.

c) **Assign air resources** per Operations/ICs strategy, tactics, & mission priorities

d) **Determine TFR requirements**: Vertical and horizontal dimensions. If needed, order through dispatcher or Air Operations Director.

e) **Check for airspace conflicts**: MOA's, MTR's, airports, etc.

    i) Values at risk: Life, property/structures, resources

    ii) Current fire size and potential size estimate

    iii) Fuel models and rates of spread

    iv) Fire behavior elements (wind, terrain, aspect, etc.)

f) **Recommend Strategies, Tactics, and Resources**:

    i) Direct, indirect, or parallel strategies

    ii) Target locations and priorities

    iii) Access

    iv) Anchor points

    v) Water sources

    vi) Potential helispots

    vii) Location of spot fires

    viii) Number and types of aircraft required

    ix) Use of specialized resources (helitack, rappellers, smokejumpers, and paracargo.)

g) **Provide Air Drop Information to Ground Crews**

    i) Advise personnel of impending airtanker, bucket, or paracargo drops in their work area and the need to clear the area.

ii)   If drops are near power lines, determine status of lines (live or de-energized?); Advise ground personnel of danger of being near power lines during drops.

iii)   Confirm with ground if run is to be a dry or live.

iv)   Notify ground when drop is complete and personnel can return to work area.

v)   Solicit feed back from ground crews relating to drop effectiveness.

h) **Provide Safety Oversight to Ground Crews**

i)   Monitor personnel locations relative to fire perimeter, blowup areas, etc.

ii)   Assist with locating safety zones and escape routes. Final determination must be made from ground.

iii)   Monitor weather – advises personnel of approaching fronts or thunderstorms.

iv)   Advise personnel on adverse changes in fire behavior.

v)   Direct air resources, as top priority, to protect and aid in evacuation of endangered personnel.

i) **Determine the Procedures for Ordering Tactical Aerial Resources**

i)   The authority to order retardant and helicopter support varies between dispatch centers, land status, and incident complexity. Determine the procedure before the mission begins **and confirm with the IC.**

ii)   On extended attack incidents, Division Supervisors are typically delegated the authority. However, consult with AOBD/OSC. Ensure the procedure is stated clearly in the IAP.

iii)   On initial attack incidents, the IC makes aircraft orders. The IC may choose to delegate this to the aerial supervisor. Confirm it before ordering.

5) Coordination with Dispatch

The following information should be given to dispatch in a timely manner:

a) A fire size up including a center point.

b) Horizontal and vertical dimensions of a Temporary Flight Restriction (TFR) if needed. Remember that TFRs are based on degrees, minutes, and seconds. Not decimal minutes.

c) Airspace conflicts with civilian or military aircraft.

d) The need for airtankers to load and return or hold.

e) Aircraft incidents/accidents.

f) Project needs for next day – number of aircraft by type, time requested, etc.

g) Aerial supervision flight/duty hours used and projected needs to complete the mission.

h) Request where airtankers should return over night (RON) when day's operations are completed.

i) Advise on need for aircraft maintenance and projected availability for next day.

j) Advise if airtanker has in-flight difficulty, must abort load, and return to base.

k) Advise on need for aerial supervision relief at least 2 hours before you need it.

6) Before Leaving the Incident

Before leaving the incident, the aerial supervisor will:

a) Coordinate with the Lead, ASM, ATGS or HLCO to ensure continuity of aerial supervision.

   i) Notify Operations of ETD, and who will supervise air operations.

   ii) Notify air resources of ETD and whom they will report to.

   iii) Notify the IC, Operations/Air Operations, DIVS, helibase, Lead, ASM, and HLCO when departing.

   iv) Notify dispatch of ETE to base.

   v) If you are on the last shift of the day:

      (1) Plan your release to allow for return within legal daylight flight restrictions (not necessary for twin-engine aircraft).

      (2) Update Operations personnel on fire status.

      (3) Remind remaining resources of daylight restrictions.

      (4) Confirm with dispatch status of air resources – RON or return to home base. Inform air resources of their status.

7) Post Mission Procedures

Upon return to base, do the following as appropriate to the incident:

a) Confirm need for aerial supervision aircraft for next day and notify pilot of time, etc.

b) Debrief with available air resources (ATGS pilot, airtanker pilots, HLCO, Leadplane pilot, ASM, and helicopter pilots).

c) Debrief with AOBD and dispatch.

d) Attend or provide input to incident planning meeting for next day's operations.

e) Request and review Incident Action Plan and map for next day's operation.

f) Complete payment documents.

g)   Submit SAFECOMs as required.

h)   Update logbook.

8) Emergency Procedures

a)   **Flight Emergencies** – When a flight emergency is declared, possibly as "Mayday, Mayday, Mayday" the aerial supervisor manages the emergency using appropriate procedures from the list below:

    i)   Emergency is highest priority until aircraft lands safely.

    ii)   Determine pilot's intentions for managing situation.

    iii)   Clear the airspace for the pilot as needed.

    iv)   Dedicate and clear a frequency for the emergency.

    v)   Direct the aircraft to depart mission area and climb to a safe altitude.

    vi)   Jettison load in remote areas (or specified jettison areas) if feasible.

    vii)   If problem persists, instruct aircraft to return to base or alternate landing site.

    viii)   Alert incident medevac units.

    ix)   Prepare for suppression of a fire associated with an aircraft crash.

    x)   Notify dispatch or airport tower for necessary crash/rescue protocol.

b)   **Missing Aircraft and Aircraft Mishap** – When an aircraft crash has occurred or an aircraft is missing, on scene aerial supervision manages situation using appropriate procedures below:

    i)   Assign aircraft as needed to conduct search.

    ii)   Determine location. Monitor ELT frequency (121.5) if crash site is not known or if the aircraft is missing and its status is unknown.

    iii)   Assign remaining aircraft to holding areas or return to base.

    iv)   Activate incident medevac plan through medical unit.

    v)   Assign on-site aircraft and personnel to control aircraft fire and initiate life saving measures if they can do so without jeopardizing their own safety.

    vi)   Advise IC/Operations – be discreet about aircraft and flight crew identity.

    vii)   Consider suspending non-essential aircraft operations.

    viii)   Direct ground resources to crash site.

    ix)   Direct air support operations.

c)   **Medevac of Incident Personnel** – Consider the following as appropriate:

    i)   Serve as a relay between accident site, helibase, and medical personnel.

ii)   Determine accident site location – latitude and longitude.

iii)   Obtain Medevac helicopter frequency – may be listed in Medevac Plan.

iv)   Assist rescue personnel with helispot location, etc.

v)   Provide helispot dust abatement with helicopter buckets as needed.

vi)   Guide Medevac helicopter to accident site.

Note: Incident Management Teams typically have an established procedure for incidents within the incident (IWI). Obtain a briefing from Air Ops.

This page intentionally left blank.

Chapter 8 – Aerial Firefighting Strategy and Tactics

Principles that apply to ground operations also apply to air operations. Strategies are based on values at risk and resource management objectives, while tactics are based on fuel type, fire intensity, rate of spread, resource availability, and estimated line production rate.

As an Aerial Supervisor, you will be making mainly tactical decisions based on objectives developed by incident command personnel. The most effective aerial tactic is anchor, flank and pinch.

Remember: Aerial application of suppressants and retardants will be ineffective without ground support and an anchor point.

1) Aerial Fire Suppression Strategies

There are three general suppression strategies:

a)   Direct attack – Drops next to fire edge in support of ground forces.

b)   Parallel attack – Generally parallel to and within a hundred feet of perimeter. Anticipates lateral fire spread, worker comfort/safety, and line construction rates. Multiple parallel drops can be used on unburned fuels of fast moving high intensity fires to increase line width.

c)   Indirect attack – Pre-treatment of fuels which are far removed from the main fire. Examples include safety zones, ridgelines, roads, or areas or light/sparse fuels.

2) Aerial Fire Suppression Tactics

In support of direct attack strategies, place drops where ground support is available and containment or extinguishment is likely. Direct attack the head when you are assured you won't be outflanked, fire behavior is low to moderate, and your initial load has a good chance of achieving the objective. Indirect and parallel attack strategies require coordination with ground personnel as to the timing of firing operations, structure protection, etc. Consider the following patterns and considerations.

a)   **Box and "V" Pattern** (Relatively flat terrain) – A single airtanker often can make multiple drops forming a retardant line around a small fire or "V" off the head or heel.

b)   **Parallel or Stacking Pattern** (Steep Ground) – When steep terrain precludes boxing a fire, flight routes must be contoured to the slope. Generally, drops are started at the top and progress to bottom of the fire.

c)   **Full Coverage Drop** (Delayed attack fires and spot fires) – To control fire intensity and spread, **drops should blanket the entire fire**. Multiple drops may be required to get a heavy coverage level. On small fires the chance of a partial hit on the first drop is significant. It is wise to drop a partial load on the first pass. The experience of the first drop plus feedback from the ATGS and the ground will likely increase the accuracy on the next drop.

3) General Tactical Considerations

Tactical plans are based on the chosen strategy and a working knowledge of the following principles. The following will help in developing and carrying out an aerial tactical plan.

a) **Simplicity & Flexibility** – Stick to a few basic tactical objectives. Be ready to change priorities as needed to achieve strategic objectives.

b) **Retardant Versus Water or Foam** – Unless there are environmental constraints, retardant application may be preferred compared to the use of water or foam. If long term retardant is required, don't rely on water or foam – they normally require immediate (0-30 minute) follow up.

c) **Proper Coverage Level** – Use the proper coverage level for the fuel types.

d) **Dense Canopies** – Multiple drops may be required to penetrate canopies and treat surface fuels with proper coverage level.

e) **Sustained Attack** – To effectively lay a retardant line under normal fire conditions, continuous drops supported by ground forces are required. Calculate turn-around time and order enough aircraft to maintain a sustained attack.

f) **Use Down Sun** – Avoid flight routes directly into sun on the horizon.

g) **Blow ups/Flare-ups** – Direct or parallel attack is usually ineffective. Shut down operations until conditions are more favorable or concentrate on pre-treatment targets.

h) **Target Priorities** – Retardant use is usually prioritized in the following order:

   i) Human Safety

   ii) Structure Protection

   iii) Natural Resources

i) **Portable Retardant Plants** – Where long turn-around times or lack of large airtankers will not provide a sustained attack, consider ordering a portable retardant plant and type I /II helicopters or SEATs. SEATs typically respond with a support vehicle which has suppressant/retardant mixing/loading capabilities. Within 24-36 hours portable plants can be delivered and set up on or near an incident. Some operators can provide a module consisting of a type I helicopter, portable plant, retardant, and mixing crew. Not all retardants are approved for fixed tank helicopters. Consult the qualified products list for approved retardants.

j) **Staggered Duty Hours** – Stagger aircraft duty hours to provide availability during early morning through end of daylight.

k) **Early Morning Drops** – Often the most effective. Don't wait until it's too late to order retardant. Use drops to prevent problems, not to cure them!

l) **Wind Drift** – An increase in coverage level may be required to reduce the effects of drift. Caution – Maintain safe drop height.

m) **Critical Targets** – On initial attack incidents, identify targets for attaining quick containment and drop on these first.

n) **Anchor Points** – Work from an anchor. Re-establish the anchor if it is lost. Terrain may dictate flights are flown toward, rather than from, an anchor point.

o) **Maximize Line Production by**:

   i) Keeping lines relatively straight; minimize angles

   ii) Taking advantage of natural barriers and lighter fuels

   iii) Allowing pilot to select the best and safest flight route

p) **Gaps in Line** – Observe for gaps in retardant, foam or water line. Pickup gaps with subsequent drops or with ground resources or SEATs.

q) **Plan for Extending and Intersecting** – Plan current drops so they can be extended or intersected effectively by future drops.

r) **Anticipate Spot Fires** – Generally downwind of smoke columns.

s) **Control Fire Intensity** – With direct drops on or next to fuels. Effective only when immediately followed up by ground forces.

t) **Reduce Spotting Potential** – With pretreatment drops on fuel beds.

u) **Maintain Honest Evaluations** – To assist pilots with making corrections.

v) **Use Correct Resources**: Match resources to correct tactical objectives.

w) **Retardant Drops near Water Resources** – Agency policy and Unit level tactical plans may restrict the use of airtankers and helicopters near water resources. When drops are planned in sensitive areas, the ATGS should contact the local unit or a Resource Advisor for applicable policy restrictions, (e.g., Interagency policy prohibits dropping retardant within 300 feet of stream courses).

   i) Locate and map water resources within the tactical air operations area.

   ii) Determine safe drop distances.

   iii) Monitor wind conditions and drift and adjust restrictions as necessary.

   iv) Use helicopters to maximize drop accuracy.

4) Initial Attack and Multiple Fire Operations

a) **Assuming Control of Air Operations in Progress** – The aerial supervisor often arrives after other air resources have arrived. Before assuming control the aerial supervisor should:

i) Monitor air traffic and operation's frequencies while inbound to the incident

ii) Contact air and ground resources to determine status of air resources on-site.

iii) Allow safe operations in progress to continue temporarily.

iv) Make assessment of the incident.

v) Brief the IC of assessment and make recommendations and/or request IC's strategy and tactics and mission priorities. The experience level of an initial attack IC determines the ATGS role

vi) Establish contact with key ground operations personnel

b) **Initial Attack Mission Priorities** – Often during initial attack several aircraft arrive at the same time. Each resource has different altitude, route, and time requirements. While some missions can be done simultaneously, the confined airspace usually requires priorities be established based on:

i) **Time** – Typical time requirements for common missions are:

(1) Bucket drop: 1-2 minutes

(2) Helitack: 3-5 minutes

(3) Helicopter rappel: 20 minutes

(4) Airtanker: 7-15 minutes (one vs. multiple drops)

(5) Smokejumper: 30 minutes. (depends on number of jumpers/cargo to be dropped)

ii) **General Considerations**

(1) Which resources are ready?

(2) Can any resources be held or parked?

(3) Can any missions be done simultaneously?

(4) Can any mission be done in stages?

(5) Conditions that if delayed may preclude mission completion, i.e. fuel remaining, pilot duty/flight time remaining

iii) **Normal Priority** – Considering all factors, the normal priority is:

(1) Helicopter bucket/retardant drop

(2) Airtanker

(3) Helitack/rappel

(4) Smokejumper

c) **Initial Attack Responsibilities with no IC** – The ATGS, in consultation with dispatch, has the following responsibilities on initial attack incidents with no IC:

i) Make initial fire size up

ii) Recommend specific resources based on fire behavior, access, response time, resource availability and capability

iii) Develop tactical plan

iv) Give periodic status reports to dispatch or responding resources

v) Assist responding resources with locating the incident

vi) Brief ground resources on potential safety concerns and fire behavior

vii) Assign arriving resources based on tactical plan until a qualified IC arrives

d) **Multiple Fire Situations** – An ATGS may be activated during predicted or active lightning storms when multiple fire starts are likely to assist with:

i) Fire detection: Coordinates, legal descriptions, VOR and distance, etc.

ii) Incident priorities are based on the following:

(1) Threat to life and property

(2) Land status

(3) Fire behavior – current and expected spread

(4) Environmental sensitivity

(5) Political considerations

(6) Potential resource loss

iii) **Determine Access** – Roads, trails, distance, and time requirements.

iv) **Recommend Initial Attack Resources** – Based on resource capability, mode of access, probable availability and response time.

v) **Develop Initial Attack Strategy and Tactics** – Based on resource objectives, fire behavior, type and numbers of air and ground resources responding within specific time frames.

vi) **Direct Resources per** strategic and tactical plans until a qualified IC arrives.

vii) **Report Intelligence to** dispatch and IC.

viii) **Reassign Resources** – to higher priority incidents if they develop.

e) **Delayed Attack Fires** – When many small fires have started in a widespread area, resources are usually in short supply. An ATGS may be assigned to assess and prioritize fires. Delayed attack fires, or fires that cannot be staffed within a few hours, may require a holding action until ground resources are available. Timely drops while the fire is small can be effective in holding or containing a fire temporarily. Retardant is much more effective than water. One type II or II airtanker can make holding drops on three or four small fires. During these situations the ATGS will:

i)   Determine delayed attack fires requiring retardant. Request resources as needed

ii)   Set priorities. Consider flight time between fires. If priorities are equal, consider dropping on fires in close to each other before moving to fires some distance away.

iii)   Direct retardant drops. General covering of the entire fire is recommended when controlling both fire spread and fire intensity. While drops covering the fire reduce fire intensity, they also make burnout operations difficult if not impossible.

iv)   Monitor status of fires. Change priorities as necessary.

5) Wildland Urban Interface

Airtankers and helicopters can be effective on urban interface incidents. If improperly managed they can be a serious hazard to the public and a liability to the responsible agency. Consider the following in the urban interface:

a)   **Policy and Regulations** – Fires in the urban interface are considered to be in "congested areas." Refer to Chapter 4 for more detail

   i)   **Order a Lead/ASM** – As required under FAR 91.119 – USDA Grant of Exemption 392. Refer to Chapter 4 for specific requirements.

   ii)   **Implement a TFR** – Under 14 CFR 91.137 if the incident meets the criteria for implementation. Refer to the *Interagency Airspace Coordination Guide.*

   iii)   Assign an aerial supervisor

b)   **Urban Interface Hazards** – The following hazards to aircraft are often associated with urban interface incidents:

   i)   Dense smoke and poor visibility

   ii)   Power lines (may have to be de-energized)

   iii)   Antennas

   iv)   Tall buildings

   v)   Media aircraft

   vi)   Propane tanks

c)   **Ground Safety** – Urban interface incidents often have many citizens and homeowners scattered through the operations area. This can seriously impair tactical air operations and expose ground personnel to extreme risk.

d)   **Effectiveness of Resources** – As urbanization increases tactical effectiveness decreases. It becomes more critical that airtanker and helicopter drops be closely supervised to prevent inadvertent drops on non-incident persons and unnecessary damage to improvements. The aerial supervisor is responsible for providing the best available resources that can:

i)   Minimize risk to people and improvements.

ii)   Provided there is an adequate water source, the type 1 helicopter, with its maneuverability, drop accuracy, and quick turn-around time, is the best resource in the classic occluded urban interface.

iii)   Drops are generally not effective on structures that are burning beyond the initial start phase or if the fire is inside the structure.

e)   **Urban Interface Tactical Planning Principles** – Apply the following principles in developing the tactical plan and making air resource assignments:

     i)   Assess the situation and identify the following:

         (1)   Identify air operational hazards

         (2)   Locate non-incident people in operations area

         (3)   Protection of evacuation routes

         (4)   Triage structures

         (5)   Identify possible dipsites and portable retardant plant sites

         (6)   Determine how air resources can best support suppression objectives

     ii)   Request electrical transmission lines are de-energized. Don't assume that they will be. Warn ground personnel not to be under or near power lines during drops.

     iii)   Determine where airtankers or helicopters can be most effective.

     iv)   Recommend location of portable retardant or water dipsites.

     v)   Use airtankers in areas where visibility, hazards, flight routes, crowd control and target selection ensure reasonable effectiveness and acceptable risk.

     vi)   Use helicopters on targets requiring more maneuverability and accuracy under conditions that would preclude safe and effective airtanker operations.

     vii)   When possible, avoid holding patterns with airtankers over populated areas.

This page intentionally left blank.

Chapter 9 – Tactical Aircraft Operations

1) Low Level Operations (Lead/ASM)

Low level flight operations involve fixed wing aircraft flying below 500' above ground level (AGL). These missions are typically performed in order to ensure airtanker drop effectiveness and safety. Aircraft and flight crews are specially trained and authorized for low level missions. Situational awareness is the responsibility of each Lead/ASM crew member to ensure safe flight operations. The Lead/ASM conducts these operations in the following manner:

a) Lead/ASM Tactical Flight Checklists

Lead/ASM aircraft are configured for tactical flight operations in accordance with the checklist specific to the aircraft being flown. The flight crew completes tactical checklists before conducting low level flight.

i) High Level Reconnaissance

(1) A high recon pass is executed prior to descending to low level.

(2) Look for aircraft over the incident including media and non-participating aircraft.

(3) Analyze the terrain. Identify potential approach and departure paths while identifying prominent target features. Fly the patterns at an altitude to detect hazards. Study the lay of the land to establish emergency exits.

ii) Low Level Reconnaissance

(1) Obtain clearance from ATGS for low level operations.

(2) Check for turbulence, hazards to low level flight, and low level target identification features.

(3) Fly the emergency exit paths to locate potential hazards not identified from a higher level.

b) Tactical Flight Profiles

i) Show me Profile – A Show me profile is a low level pass made over the target using the physical location of the aircraft to demonstrate the line and start point of the retardant drop. The Show-Me Profile is normally used for the first airtanker on a specific run or when an incoming airtanker has not had the opportunity to observe the previous drop. A Show-Me can be used alone or before other profiles.

The pilot begins the run when the airtanker crew can visually identify the aircraft, hazards, line, start and exit point of the drop.

Figure 5. Show-Me Profile

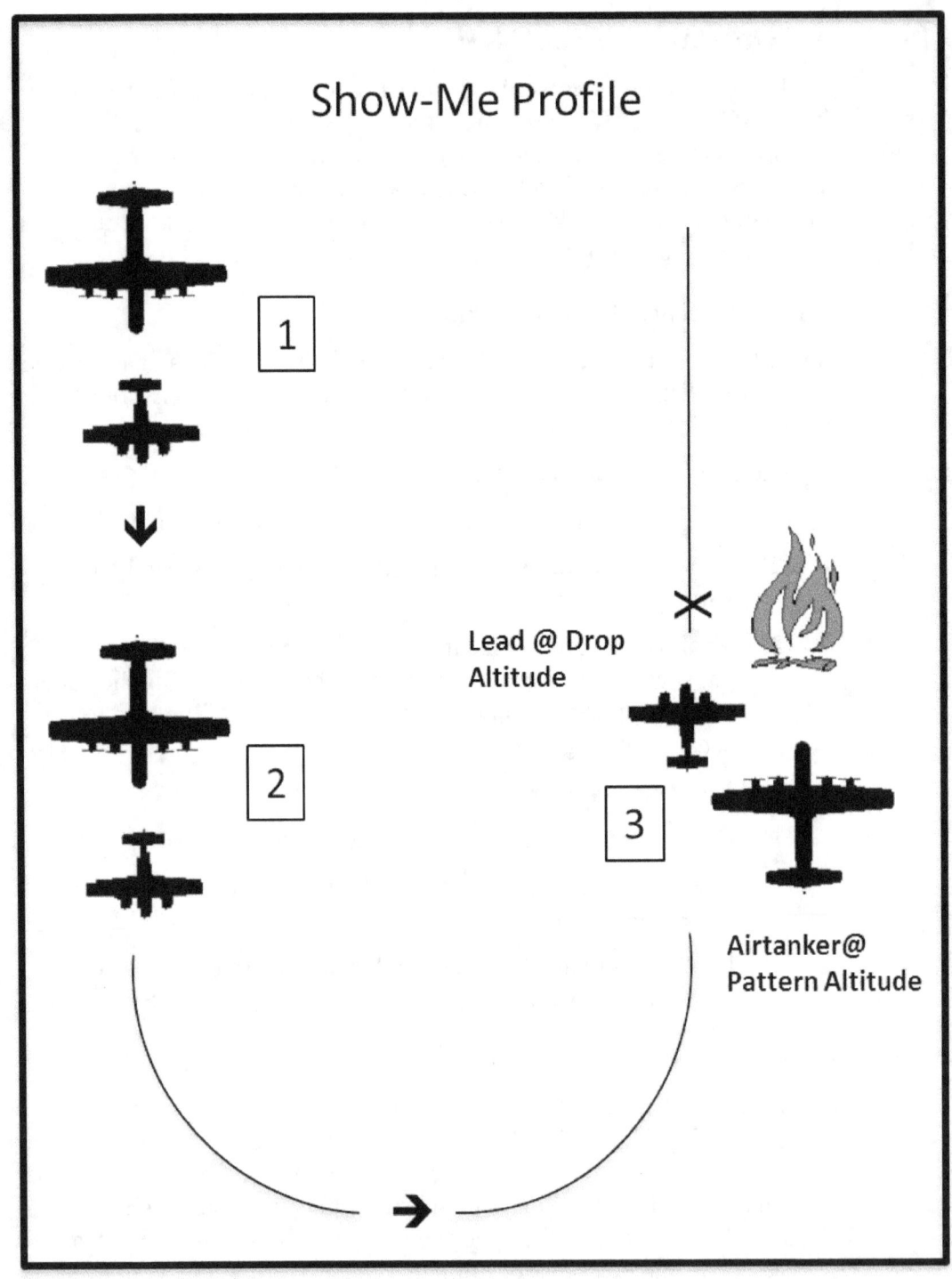

Show-Me Profile

Lead @ Drop Altitude

Airtanker@ Pattern Altitude

ii) **Chase Position Profile** – The Chase Position Profile is an observation position in trail of and above the airtanker at a position of 5 to 7 o'clock. The Chase Position Profile is used to verbally confirm or adjust the position of the airtanker when on final, and to evaluate the drop.

Figure 6. Chase Position Profile

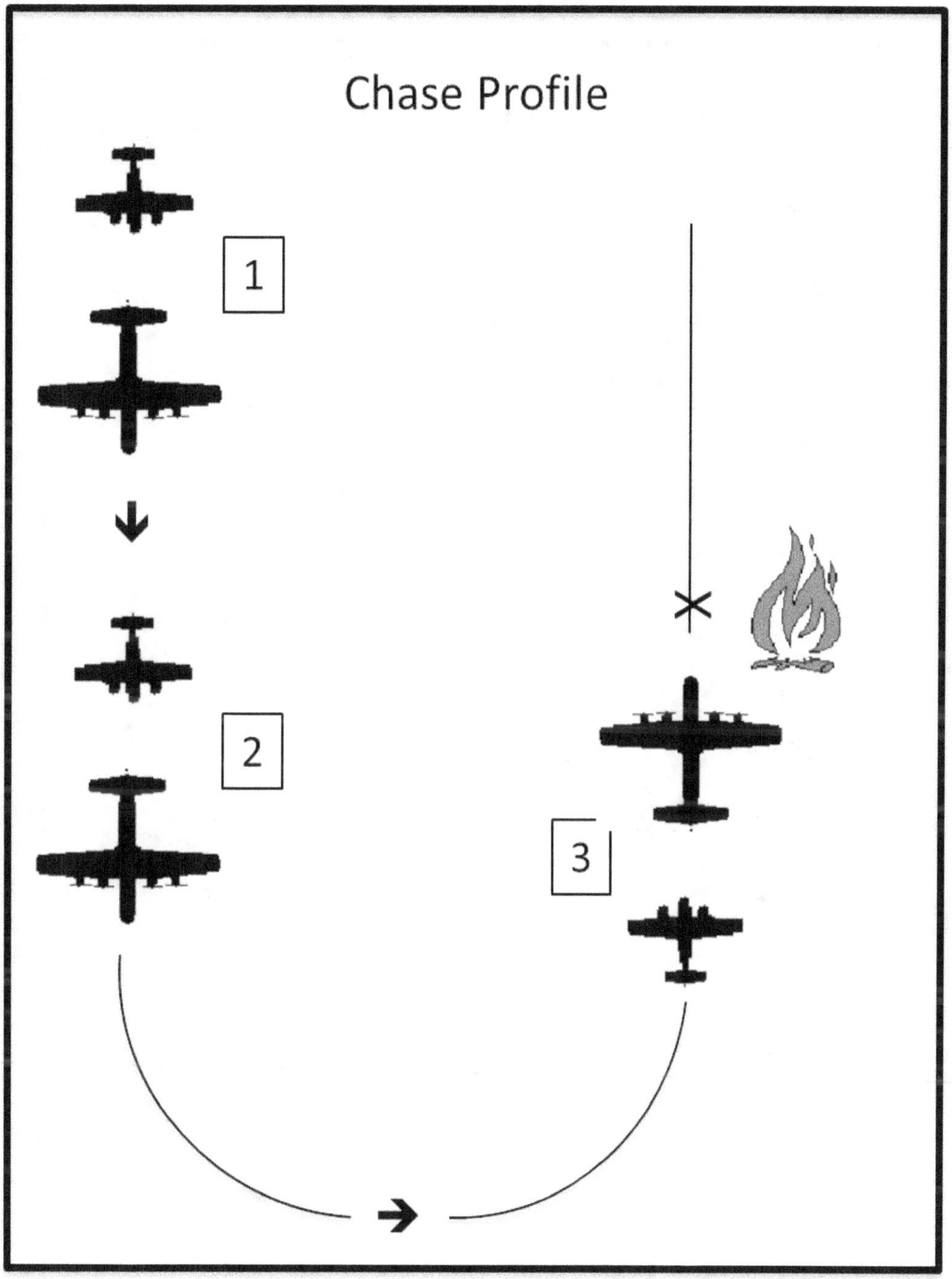

i)   **Lead Profile** – The Lead profile is a low level (below 500' AGL) airtanker drop pattern, made with the Leadplane approximately 1/4 mile ahead of the airtanker. The Lead Profile is used at the request of the Airtanker Crew, or when the line or start point is difficult to see or to describe due to lack of visibility or references.

Figure 7. Lead Profile

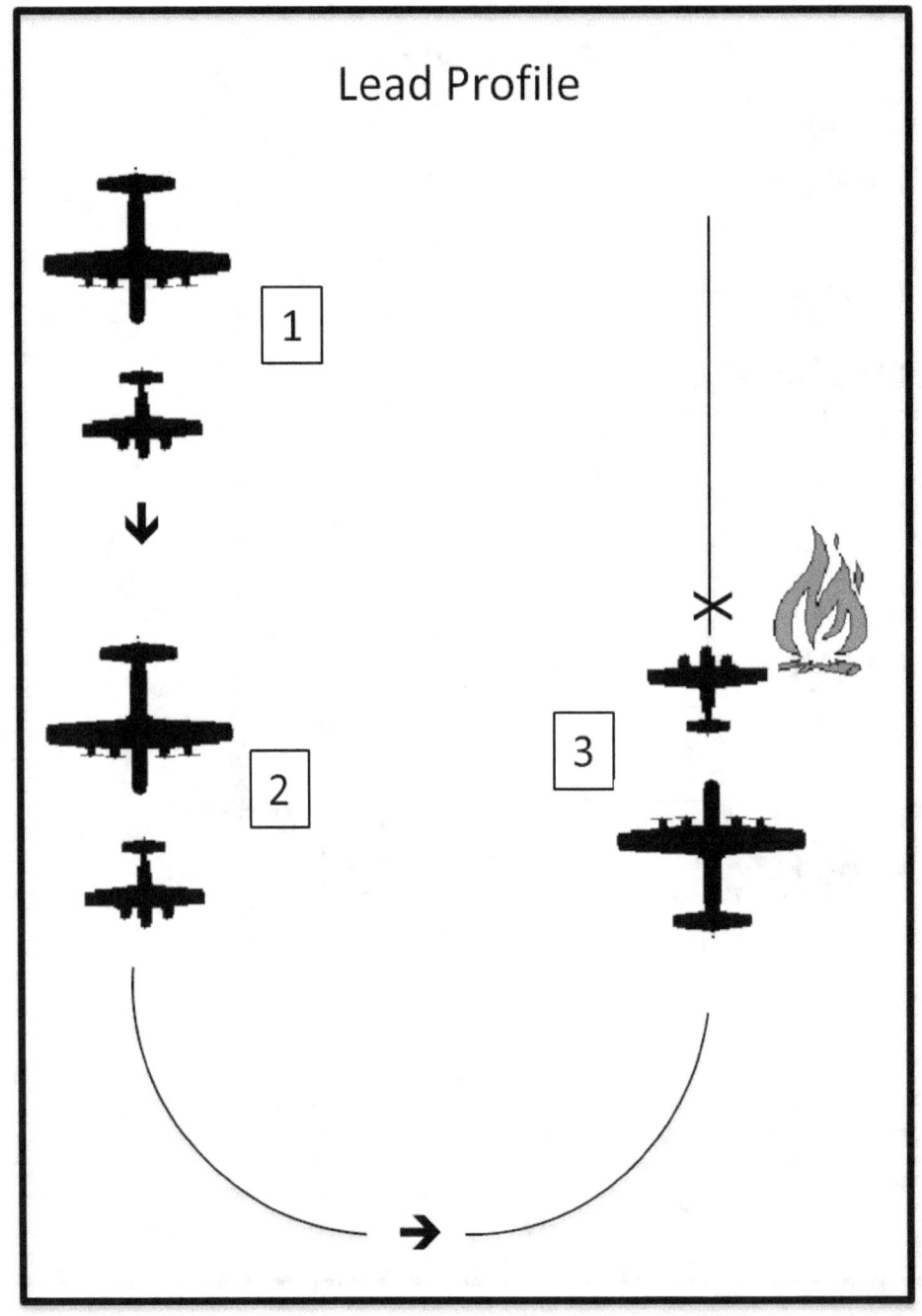

c) Airtanker Briefings

i) **Initial Briefing** – This briefing should be accomplished when the tanker makes the initial contact. The initial briefing shall include:

    (1) **Initial Positioning** – Define the location you want the airtanker to fly to upon arriving at the incident. Include information on other aircraft at that location and their assigned altitude(s). It is helpful to identify the specific airtanker they will be sequenced to drop after.

    (2) This location may be a holding pattern, a general point on or adjacent to the incident, or a specific location on the incident. These locations may be defined as a prominent geographic feature (lake, mountain peak, river, island, valley, etc), a cardinal compass position, or a fire related position (left flank, head, etc.).

    (3) **Altitude/Altimeter Setting** – Assign the altitude to come into the incident airspace at and give the altimeter setting.

    (4) **Altitude** – Define a hard altitude or a "block altitude" for the airtanker to arrive over the initial point. Be cognizant of performance limitations of the airtanker make and model. One can assign interval altitudes for aircraft to hold in a holding pattern. The preferred method is for the airtankers to work with each other for separation in a holding pattern or area. If this method is used, the reporting airtankers need to be directed to contact other aircraft in the holding area to coordinate their arrival.

    (5) **Altimeter Setting** – The altimeter setting can be updated periodically by obtaining information from arriving airtankers. Changes in altimeter settings on an incident must be confirmed by a "read back" from **all** incident aircraft.

    (6) **Hazards** – Identify general hazards (weather, turbulence, visibility, towers/power lines, etc.).

    (7) **Portion of Load and Coverage Level** – Specify the portion of the load by fractions to be dropped (1/4, 1/3 1/2, whole load; or identify that start/stop points will be defined in the target description). Coverage level is expressed by numerical values beginning with one. It is important to know what type of retardant the airtanker is carrying, as this will influence configuration and coverage levels.

    Note: When an ATGS is assigned to the incident, they are responsible for determining (with input from the incident commander) the coverage level unless this is delegated to the Leadplane pilot.

ii) **Tactical Briefing** – This briefing should be conducted when the airtanker is established in a position to view the intended target. The tactical briefing shall include:

(1) **Target Description** – A proven method of describing a target is to start with a large geographic area and work it down to the specific point(s). A well-defined drop start point is critical.

(2) **Objective** – Time permitting, specific objective(s) of the upcoming run or series of runs clarify the methodology of the tactics being deployed and aid in defining the target.

(3) **Drop Heading and Altitude(s)** – Provide the final heading for the run and the altitude for the drop start point. It is sometimes advantageous to provide intermediate crossing altitudes (i.e. ridge/saddle crossing altitudes). The Leadplane pilot can suggest a flight path but the final decision rests with the airtanker pilot. Adhere to restrictions that may be imposed by the ATGS. These restrictions should be pre-agreed upon so that the tactical use of aircraft maximizes safety and efficiency.

Note: When working under an ATGS, it is important to utilize airspace designated for airtanker use by the ATGS for flight paths and exits. Deviations, except in emergencies, shall be cleared with the ATGS prior to maneuvering.

(4) **Hazards** – Identify specific hazards that may be encountered on the actual run.

(5) **Exit** – Brief both a normal and emergency exit. The normal exit accounts for both safety and efficiency when considering additional runs or expeditious egress from the incident to the reload base. The emergency exit addresses contingencies needed to deal with aircraft problems, such as an engine failure, tank malfunctions, etc. and takes advantage of the lowest terrain for the exit. Again, the Leadplane pilot can suggest exit paths but the final decision rests with the airtanker pilot.

(6) **Drop Clearance** – Issue a drop clearance prior to authorizing a low-level run. This clearance is specified as, clear to drop, live run, or dry run.

iii) **Departure Briefing**

(1) **Drop Evaluation** – Be objective and address the load, not your drop. Be specific on where the load went (the retardant line started too early/late, left/right of the target, etc). It is not helpful or appreciated by the industry to say good drop on every drop.

(2) **Reload Instructions** – Find out ahead of time from the Incident Commander, ATGS, and dispatch what they want the airtanker to do. It is well within your purview to recommend courses of action but the decision rests with the above-mentioned positions. Solicit from the airtanker pilot any information that will affect their timing and return to the incident or where they are to go and reload or hold (fuel status, days off, ground support needs, etc.).

(3) **Dispatch/ATGS** – Notify dispatch of the airtankers departure, ETE to base, and instructions (load and return, load and hold, released, etc.)

Note: If an ATGS is working the incident, inform them of the completion of the final drop and obtain reload instructions. The ATGS will normally handle communications with dispatch unless otherwise delegated.

d) Maneuvering

When leading airtankers, shallow to medium banked turns no greater than 30 degrees should be used. On occasion, the possibility may exist where terrain or conditions dictate maneuvering at values greater than the standard 30 degrees. In such circumstances, angles of bank up to, but not exceeding, 45 degrees are acceptable. Inform the airtanker pilot ahead of time if turns in excess of 30 degrees are anticipated. Airspeed control is critical to a safe pattern. The shape, airspeed, and size of the pattern shall be well planned to minimize the airtanker pilot's maneuvering workload.

i) **Minimum Airspeed** – Airspeed during normal Leadplane operations shall not be flown below best single engine rate of climb airspeed (Vyse) or minimum controllable airspeed one engine inoperative (Vmca). Refer to agency specific aircraft flight operations handbooks or pilot operating handbooks.

ii) **Approach and Descent to the Target** – The run should be downhill, down canyon, down sun with the greatest degree of safety in mind. Maintain the agreed upon airspeed in order to sustain approximately 1/4 mile separation between the Leadplane and airtanker. A descending approach with a constant rate of descent is desired, terrain permitting. Brief the airtanker pilot ahead of time if special maneuvering is anticipated. Advise the airtanker of hazards (i.e. turbulence, down air, restrictions to visibility, obstacles, etc.).

iii) **Final Approach to the Target** – Power up and clean up drag devices (when applicable) to cross the target area not less than 130 KIAS. Do not accelerate too soon and run away from the airtanker.

iv) **Drop Height** – The minimum is 150 feet above the top of the vegetation for heavy tankers. SEATs drop at 60 feet. It is important for the retardant to "rain" vertically with little or no forward movement. The airtanker pilot is responsible for maintaining safe drop heights.

v) **Over the Target** – Identify the start point with a verbal, "Here."

vi) **Exiting the Target** – Comply with the briefed exit instructions. When possible, turn off the centerline of the run before initiating a climb or pull-up maneuver (be cognizant of the airtankers position at all times). Exiting is a critical maneuver at low altitude. Take every precaution to ensure that airspeed and aircraft attitude are within safe limits. The pull-up maneuver need not be greater than what is required to comfortably clear all obstacles and to provide the Leadplane pilot with a view of the drop for evaluation (Flight Safety has priority over drop evaluation). Airspeed shall be no less than 130 KIAS and a load factor no greater than 1.5 positive G's when exiting the target.

vii) **Emergency Overrun Procedures** – In the event of an imminent overrun of the Leadplane by the airtanker, the airtanker crew will attempt to communicate the overrun and utilize the following standard overrun procedures unless otherwise briefed:

(1) Straight out flight paths: Pass the Leadplane on the right.

(2) Left or right turn flight paths: Pass the Leadplane outside the turn.

(3) Terrain or visibility limitations: When terrain or visibility prevent utilizing 1 or 2 above, pass above the Leadplane.

2) Airtanker Operations

a) Airtanker Tactical Considerations

i) Airtanker advantages: Often reserved for initial attack because:

ii) High cruise speed: Airtankers fly fast and arrive at most fires long before helicopters can be dispatched. Airtankers may be the only aerial resource available if an incident has no dipsites or portable mixing plant options.

iii) Long range: High speeds and fuel loads allow airtankers to cover broad geographical areas. They often respond to multiple incidents on one flight.

b) Permanent Reload Bases

Airtankers are loaded at permanent bases. Portable bases able to serve all types of airtankers may be set up for special situations.

c) Factors Influencing Drop Effectiveness

A number of factors affect drop accuracy, line width and length, and coverage level required for particular fuel model and fire intensity. These factors include:

i) **Pilot Skill** – Ability to make accurate drops.

ii) **Aircraft Make and Model** – Each aircraft make and model has advantages and disadvantages in different operating environments. Performance elements include power, maneuverability, pilot's visibility and airspeed control.

iii) **Tanking, Gating or Door System** – Quantity of liquid, tank configuration, flow rate and door release mechanism.

iv) **Airtanker Drop Height** – The minimum safe drop height is 150 feet above vegetation. Normally drops are made from 150 to 250 feet above vegetation. Increased height reduces coverage level and increases line width. The most uniform and efficient retardant distribution is attained when near vertical fall of the retardant occurs. The optimum drop height is when the momentum of the load stops its forward trajectory and begins to fall vertically. SEAT drop height 60 feet is above vegetation.

v) **Airtanker Speed** – Airtanker drops, depending on the type of aircraft, range from 120-140 knots. Faster speeds generally reduce peak coverage levels, increase pattern momentum, and increase low coverage length.

vi) **Diving vs. Climbing** – A diving maneuver tends to shorten the pattern and increase coverage levels. Conversely, a rising maneuver tends to toss or loft retardant and elongate the pattern.

vii) **Wind** – The effect of wind is to deflect retardant and greatly increase the pattern's fringe area. The effectiveness of retardant/water drops should be closely evaluated when wind velocities reach 15 kts. Retardant drops are generally not effective in winds 25 kts or greater.

   (1) Headwind: The effect of dropping into the wind is to shorten the line length and increase coverage level.

   (2) Crosswind drops will result in increased line width and cover a larger area at reduced coverage levels.

viii) **Flame Lengths** – Direct Attack with retardants at the prescribed coverage level is generally effective in flame lengths up to 4 feet. Flame lengths from 4 to 8 feet require increasingly higher coverage levels. Retardant, unless applied in heavy coverage levels and greater widths, is not generally effective when flame lengths are greater than 8 feet. Long term retardant is most effective when applied to available fuels outside of the fire perimeter.

ix) **Canopy Density** – Drops in timber or fuel models with a dense concentration of tall trees are often ineffective. Canopy interception significantly reduces penetration to ground fuels. An open canopy allows for better penetration.

x) **Availability of Ground Forces** – Except in light fuels where extinguishing the fire with retardant may be possible, the ATGS must determine if ground forces will be able to take advantage of the retardant within a reasonable time.

d) **Retardant Coverage Levels**

Coverage level refers to the number of gallons of retardant applied on fuels per 100 square feet. Fire scientists have determined how many gallons per 100 square feet (GPC) it takes to effectively retard flammability in fuel models under normal flame lengths. Coverage levels range from .5 to greater than 8. The ATGS instructs airtanker pilots to make drops at specific coverage levels.

Recommended Coverage Levels – The chart below identifies the recommended coverage level for each fuel model. The coverage level may need to be increased under more adverse burning conditions or when retardant does not effectively penetrate a heavy tree canopy.

Table 9. Recommended Retardant Coverage Levels			
Coverage Level	**NFDRS Fuel Model**	**NFFL FB Fuel Model**	**Fuel Model Description**
1	A,L,S	1	Annual Perennial Western Grasses, Tundra
2	C	2	Conifer with Grass, Shortneedle Closed Conifer, Summer Hardwood
	H,R	8	
	E,P,U	9	Longneedle Conifer, Fall Hardwood
2 or 3	T	2	Sagebrush with Grass
3	N	3	Sawgrass
	F	5	Intermediate Brush (green)
	K	11	Light Slash
4	G	10	Shortneedle Conifer (heavy dead litter)
6	O	4	Southern Rough
	F,Q	6	Intermed. Brush (cured), Black Spruce
Greater Than 6	B,O	4	California Mixed Chaparral; High Pocosin
	J	12	Medium Slash
	I	13	Heavy Slash

e) **Airtanker Drop Patterns**

By opening one or more doors simultaneously or in quick succession, a variety of patterns and coverage levels can be achieved. The ATGS must know the number of doors that can be dropped singly or in combination, various drop pattern options, and the coverage level required for various fuel models.

i) **Salvo Drop** – One or more doors are opened simultaneously. Generally used on small targets such as spot fires or targets requiring heavy coverage levels. Rarely is a full salvo ordered.

ii) **Trail Drop** – With multiple tank systems, two or more doors are open sequentially and at specified intervals giving continuous overlapping flow over a desired distance at the required coverage level. The same result is obtained with constant flow systems by opening the doors partially.

f) Heavy Airtanker Line Length Production Table

This chart displays line production by coverage level and gallons dropped for drops made at the recommended drop height and airspeed. The chart should be used as a general guide and will need to be adjusted for specific tank systems, airtanker make and model and the actual drop conditions.

Table 10. Heavy Airtanker Line Length Production Chart (feet)							
Volume Dropped (Gallons)	Coverage Level 0.5	Coverage Level 1	Coverage Level 2	Coverage Level 3	Coverage Level 4	Coverage Level 6	Coverage Level 8
800	2,246	1,114	526	311	189	38	0
1,000	2,337	1,202	607	384	255	90	0
1,200	2,429	1,289	687	458	321	142	9
1,400	2,520	1,377	768	531	387	194	46
1,600	2,611	1,465	848	604	454	245	84
1,800	2,702	1,552	929	678	520	297	121
2,000	2,794	1,640	1,009	751	586	349	158
2,200	2,885	1,728	1,090	824	652	400	196
2,400	2,976	1,815	1,170	897	718	452	233
2,600	3,068	1,903	1,251	971	784	504	270
2,800	3,159	1,991	1,331	1,044	850	556	308
3,000	3,250	2,078	1,411	1,117	916	607	345

g) Ten Principles of Retardant Application

i) Determine the strategy; direct or indirect, based on fire size up and resources available

ii) Establish an anchor point and work from it

iii) Use the proper drop height

iv) Apply proper coverage levels

v) Drop down hill always; down sun when feasible

vi) Drop into the wind for best accuracy

vii) Maintain honest evaluation and effective communication between the ground and air

viii) Use direct attack only when ground support is available or extinguishment is feasible

ix) Plan drops so that they can be extended or intersected effectively.

x) Monitor retardant effectiveness and adjust its use accordingly

h) SEAT Operational Principles

i) Minimum SEAT drop height is 60' above vegetation.

ii) SEAT operations have a wind restriction: Sustained at 30 kts or a 15 kt gust spread.

iii) Get them flying early – SEATs are most effective on small, emerging incidents

iv) Keep them flying – Reduce turnaround times by setting up a remote reload base as close as possible to the incident

v) Utilize aerial supervision – Efficiency is maximized when time spent over the target is minimized. Leadplanes typically utilize the show me and chase profiles

vi) Integrate SEATs with other resources – Use SEATs in conjunction with helicopters and heavy tankers

vii) Work SEATs in groups to minimize line length

viii) Use retardant or suppressants with SEATs- Foam and Gels work well for direct attack

ix) SEATs are not heavy tankers. The max coverage level from a SEAT is 4.

x) SEAT pilots are trained to apply the **ASHE** acronym for safe operations:

(1) **Approach**

(2) **Speed**

(3) **Height**

(4) **Exit**

i) Airtanker Flight Routes

i) **Route Safety** – Approaches and exits must allow for a level or downhill flight maneuver. No uphill flight routes for airtankers!

ii) **Visibility** – Poor visibility from smoke or sun may preclude using the safest and most effective route. Alternate routes may be acceptable, but may result in less effective drops.

3) Helicopter and Helitanker Operations

Helicopter Tactical Considerations

a) Helicopter Advantages

Helicopters are often a very cost effective resource on extended attack and project incidents because of the following:

b) Short Turnaround Times

A type I helicopter with a 3-minute turn-around can deliver upwards of 45,000 gallons per hour (Boeing 234, S-64). By comparison a type I airtanker will typically deliver 2000 to 3000 gallons per hour based on a one-hour turn-around.

c)   Low Speed and Drop Accuracy

The ability to do hover or low speed drops makes helicopters very accurate if flown by an experienced pilot. Helicopters are an excellent choice for; targets in confined airspaces in steep and dissected terrain, small targets where airtanker drops may be wasted by covering a larger than required area, to treat gaps in airtankers line, in low visibility situations (smoke, low ceiling) where airtankers cannot fly, near water resources to minimize the potential for water contamination, and in the urban interface environment where accuracy is paramount. Caution – Drops on steep slopes may dislodge rocks onto crews below.

d)   Dipsites

For an effective helicopter operation, good water sources are required. Sources can include wide mouth portable tanks. The ATGS should inventory suitable dipsites. Following are considerations:

i)   Approaches should be into wind. Determine if wind direction is the same at hover level as it is at the dipsite level when using a longline.

ii)   Helicopters equipped with a tank and snorkel require water depth of 18 inches to 3 feet for hover filling.

iii)   Be aware of any local resource concerns and fire management plan restrictions – ask the local fire managers and/or dispatch for specifics.

iv)   Approach, departure, and dipsite must be free of hazards.

v)   Avoid fast moving streams and rivers.

vi)   Avoid contamination of water resources from buckets or snorkels that have previously been used in foam or retardant dipsites and/or any other resource contamination concerns (i.e. Whirling disease).

vii)   On private lands, attempt to secure permission from the landowner before using a private water source. This may be addressed in a pre-attack plan. Anticipate the need and secure permission before the need arises.

viii)   Utilize dipsite managers (when available) to provide an added margin of safety at established dipsites.

e)   Longline Bucket Operations

i)   Effective for dipping out of close quarters (ex. dipsite surrounded by tall timber)

ii)   Reduce rotor wash on the fire

iii)   Effective for filling portable tanks

iv) **Establish Direct Communications Between Helicopters and Ground Contacts** – If Air-to-Ground is too congested; assign Division frequencies for direct communications between ground contact and helicopters.

v) **Allow Pilots to Select Drop Approach**

   (1) Cross-slope, usually most preferred

   (2) Down slope, second choice

   (3) Upslope or downwind, least desirable approach

f) **Helicopter Utilization by Type**

   i) Type II and III helicopters can work together but do not integrate Type I helicopters unless all pilots involved are comfortable with pattern and separation.

   ii) Type I and II helicopters can be effective for line production.

   iii) Use type III helicopters on isolated targets requiring lower volumes of water.

   iv) **Helicopter Drop Height** – Critical in terms of accuracy, effectiveness, and effect of rotor wash on fire behavior. Look for flare-ups after drops.

g) **Helicopter Delivery Systems**

Some systems can regulate flow rate and are capable of multiple or partial drops. Many helicopters are equipped with units for injecting foam into the bucket or tank.

   i) **Buckets:** Two basic types of bucket are currently being used:

   (1) Rigid Shell Buckets – Some capable of multiple drops

   (2) Collapsible buckets (and foldable) - Some capable of single drop only

   ii) **Fixed Tanks** – A variety of tank systems have been developed by different operators and agencies. Most these can be quickly attached to the fuselage. The tanks are generally filled using a snorkel while the helicopter is hovering over a water source. The tank can also be filled on the ground using standard cam-lock hardware. Minimum water depth requirements for the snorkel fill system are 18 inches to 3 feet. (Ex., S-64 Sky Crane with a 2500 gallon tank, foam injection, hover fills from 18 inches in 45 seconds, and provides prescribed coverage level from metered flow door system). **Helicopters:** Height is critical in terms of accuracy, effectiveness, and effect of rotor wash on fire behavior. Helicopter must be high enough to not cause flare-ups. Forward air speed results in less rotor wash. Type 1 helicopters, even with a 200 foot longline, produce strong rotor wash.

Note: Caution when mixing multiple helicopters with dissimilar delivery systems (i.e. Belly Hooked Bucket, Longline and Tanked Aircraft). Different airspeed, maneuverability, flight profile and pilot site picture have potential to impact aircraft separation.

h)   Helicopter Drop Patterns

In a hover a helicopter can deliver a salvo drop, while in forward flight it can deliver a trail drop.

4) Smokejumper Operations

Consider ordering jumpers early. Quick arrival of personnel can be essential in catching a fire. Ram-air smokejumpers can be deployed in winds up to 30 mph. The smokejumper spotter will determine if conditions are appropriate.

BLM smokejumper aircraft are dispatched with a standard load of 8 jumpers and equipment to be self-sufficient for 48 hours. A typical mission takes 30 minutes over a fire. A spotter (senior smokejumper in charge of smokejumper missions) serves as the mission coordinator which may include coordinating the airspace over a fire until aerial supervision (ATGS/ASM/Lead) arrives.

a)   **Approach to the Fire** – Smokejumper aircraft normally approach the fire at 1500 feet AGL (streamer drop altitude for both the BLM and Forest Service).

b)   **Drop Mission** – The drop mission is a four- part operation and takes 15-40 minutes depending on the number of jumpers being deployed. Erratic winds, changing fire behavior, and other factors can extend this time.

c)   **Jump Spot Selection** – Selecting a safe jump spot sometimes requires the smokejumper airplane to make a low level pass at approximately 500 feet AGL to identify potential hazards. Letting the smokejumper aircraft orbit above other tactical aircraft to view the fire area if the lower airspace is being utilized can save time. Jumpers can also be deployed a short distance from the fire in order to conduct simultaneous tactical operations.

d)   **Streamer Runs** – The smokejumper aircraft will usually initiate a left hand pattern over the selected jump spot at a minimum of 1500 feet AGL (measured from the jumper release point). One to three streamer passes are conducted to verify the wind direction and speed.

e)   **Jump Runs** – Smokejumpers are deployed in one to four person sticks depending on the size of the spot, wind, and the aircraft. Depending on the parachute system being used, jump runs will be conducted at either 1500 feet AGL (Forest Service round parachutes) or 3000 feet AGL (BLM square parachutes). Mixed loads can vary but the standard practice is to deploy the Forest Service jumpers using the 1500' AGL pattern and then climbs to the 3000' AGL pattern for the BLM jumpers.

f)   **Cargo Runs** – After the jumpers are verified safely on the ground, the airplane descends to drop the paracargo. Cargo run patterns are similar in altitude to retardant drops, 150 to 200 feet over the drop point. The number of passes depends on the number of jumpers deployed, size of spot, and equipment needed. Runs vary from 1 pass to 10 or more. The spotter will notify the ATGS or Leadplane of the number of passes anticipated and when the mission is completed.

g) **Considerations** – Priorities vary on deploying resources on incidents but it is advisable to get the firefighters on the ground as soon as possible. Unless extenuating circumstances dictate otherwise, let the smokejumper airplane come in and perform the entire 4-part operation. If it is necessary to break into the mission to deploy other tactical aircraft, interrupt the smokejumper operation between the jump spot selection and streamer run, or between the last jump run and first paracargo run. Keep in mind that the jumpers need their tools to be effective.

When other priorities and congested airspace are an issue, consider deploying the jumpers preferably using non-conflicting flight patterns or when this is not practical, a short distance from the fire.

5) Helicopter Rappel Operations

Type 2 and 3 helicopters are used for rappelling by the U.S. Forest Service, National Park Service, and BLM. Type 3s normally carry 2 rappelers and a spotter; Type 2's, up to 6 rappelers and a spotter. The mission performed is the same as smokejumpers, initial attack and tactical support missions on large fires.

a) **Arrival** – Rappel helicopters approach the incident at 200 to 500 feet AGL or the altitude assigned by the aerial supervisor. Upon arrival at the incident site, they will survey the area to determine the best method to deploy the firefighters. The helicopter may or may not arrive configured to rappel. Normally, the helicopter is dispatched not configured to rappel unless they know that a rappel is necessary from intelligence provided by personnel at the site (ATGS, ASM, Leadplane, or recon aircraft). If not configured for the rappel, the helicopter will survey the rappel location and then fly to a landing site within a few miles of the incident to reconfigure for the rappel. It takes 5 to 10 minutes to reconfigure.

b) **Suitable Landing Site** – Providing there is a suitable landing site reasonably close to the incident and the terrain and vegetation between the landing site and the incident will not inordinately delay the firefighters walking to the incident, this alternative will be used verses rappelling. **Rappel operation**: If no landing site is available, the firefighters will rappel into the incident. The helicopter will approach the selected rappel site and perform a high hover power check (above 300 feet AGL). Once this is completed, they will descend to a stationary hover position at 250 feet AGL or lower (depending on the height of the vegetation) and perform the rappel operation. It takes each set of rappelers 15 to 25 seconds to descend on the rope. Once all the rappelers are on the ground and their ropes released from the helicopter, the spotter deploys the cargo (cargo is sometimes deployed prior to the rappelers). The total time varies but normally requires between 5 to 15 minutes performing the operation (depending on the number of rappelers)

Note: Density altitude may require the helicopter to make multiple trips to deploy partial loads. The spotter will communicate this if it is a factor.

c) **Communications** – The pilot and spotter will monitor the Guard frequency at all times and the assigned tactical frequency except on occasion when deploying personnel and cargo. When the tactical frequency is very active, the rappel helicopter may request to not monitor this frequency because a sterile cockpit is essential during the actual rappel phase. **Do not** communicate with the helicopter during this phase unless there is an emergency.

d) **Considerations** – The rappel helicopter has limited fuel duration over the incident. It is helpful to survey the area prior to the arrival of the rappel helicopter in order to point out potential landing sites or to relay that there are no landing sites near the incident. If delays are anticipated or required, consider directing the helicopter to land nearby to conserve fuel. Keep in mind that it is important to get the firefighters and their tools on the incident.

6) Water Scooper Operations (CL 215/415)

a) **Airport Requirements**

i) Runway: A 5000 foot hard surface runway with a taxiway and ramp capable of supporting 36,000 lbs. is required.

ii) Fuel: The CL-215 requires 100 octane low lead (100 LL) while the CL-415 requires Jet A fuel.

iii) Foam: A supply of foam (3-55 gallon drum capacity per fuel cycle) and the necessary equipment for handling it and pumping or loading the concentrate on the aircraft should be anticipated.

b) **Scooping Site Requirements** – The water source (or pickup lake) should be a minimum of one mile long , ¼ mile wide, free of obstructions, and at least six feet deep. The scooping path does not have to be straight, as the aircraft are somewhat maneuverable while scooping. Factors such as wind, elevation, and surrounding terrain will have a bearing on water source suitability. Less than a full load can be scooped on slightly smaller lakes. Both aircraft scoop at 80 kts, are on the water for about 15 seconds, and cover a distance of about 2,000 feet.

c) **Foam Use**

i) **Concentration** – Foam can be injected into the load at a concentration of 0.3% up to 3% in some aircraft models. Useful concentrations typically range from 0.3% to 1.0%. Foam concentrations greater than 0.6% are prone to drift.

ii) **Wet Foam** – A typical method in using foam is to attack a hot fire with straight water or wet foam (0.3%)

iii) **Dripping Foam** – After a fire has been knocked down, follow up with dripping foam (0.5%).

iv) **Dry Foam** – Dry (0.6-1.0%) foam may be used instead of dripping foam after initial knockdown with wet foam.

v) **Consistency and Water Temperature** – The consistency or aeration of the foam is affected by water temperature. A slightly higher concentration may be needed for cold water and adjustments downward may be necessary for extremely warm water.

vi) **Evaluating Consistency** – Foam consistency is best evaluated by ground personnel. Drops can be evaluated from the air using visibility criteria. Wet foam is visible for about 5 minutes, dripping foam for about 15 minutes, and dry foam is visible for 30+ minutes.

vii) **Environmental Limitations**

(1) Foam is not recommended within 300' of lakes and streams.

(2) In steep drainages or sensitive areas, check local agency policy on foam use.

(3) When scooping during foam operations, some residual foam may flush out of the vent/overflow. While very diluted, some foam may be visible on the water for a short time.

(4) Obtain a briefing from the IC or responsible agency on the limitations of foam use, if any, prior to using.

(5) Rinsing Tanks: Provide for two rinse loads of water prior to departing a fire.

d) **Tactical Considerations**

i) **Tank Configuration** – The CL-215 has two compartments totaling 1400 gallons, and the CL-415 has four compartments totaling 1600 gallons. Loads can be dropped salvo, in trail, or split into separate drops. A salvo load for both airtankers is about 280' long and 65' wide. A trail drop is about 400' x 40'.

ii) **Drop Height** – Drop height ranges from 100'-150', depending on factors such as foam vs. straight water and direction of run (into wind vs. downwind).

iii) **Clearance** – When dropping near ground crews, personnel must be moved at least 200' to the side. When drops are made 1000 feet or more in advance of crews, no clearance is necessary except to confirm no one is on the line.

e) **Flight Patterns and Turnaround Times**

i) **Typical Flight Pattern** – The typical flight pattern (or circuit) is oval, with a pickup into the wind and a downwind drop on the fire. This is the most common and efficient circuit and preferred by most pilots.

ii) **Turnaround Times** – When water sources are located next to the fire, a 90-second turnaround time is possible.

  (1) **CL-215** – A rule of thumb for turnaround times for the CL-215 in an oval circuit is; turnaround time equals miles from lake to fire plus two minutes scooping (ex. 5 miles to the fire from the lake is a 7 minute turn).

  (2) **CL-415** – Typical turnaround times for the CL-415 are: 1 mile - 3 minutes, 3 miles - 4 minutes, 6 miles - 6 minutes, 10 miles - 9 minutes, and 15 miles - 12 minutes.

iii) **Alternative Flight Patterns** – If fire intensity or other reasons indicate a need for drops into the wind or crosswind, then a U-shaped circuit or a Figure 8 will be necessary. Turnaround time will be slightly longer.

f) **Fuel Cycle Duration** – Average fuel cycle is about 4 hours. A quick turn from a close lake can shorten the cycle to 3.5 hours due to increased fuel demand.

g) **Direct Attack and Initial Attack** – Scoopers are best suited for initial attack fires. They are most commonly used for direct attack on the fire's edge with drops made half-in/half-out. Like other air resources, they are most effective when worked closely with ground resources, although drops should not be delayed while waiting for ground resources. High intensity fires may require drops to be made into the wind.

h) **Parallel Attack** – In the event ground resources are delayed or drops advance faster than the crews, a parallel attack is effective. Drops should be placed parallel to the fire's edge at a distance governed by rate of spread and progression rate of ground resources. The ATGS should consider an increase in foam proportion to dripping (.5%) or dry foam (.6-.8%). If the fire does not reach the drops in 30 to 45 minutes, reinforcement drops should be made. If progress by ground crews is too slow, retardant may be a better option, with foam and water used for knockdown and cooling the line.

i) **Indirect Attack** – While many scooping aircraft can be loaded with retardant at a tanker base, they are not designed to efficiently and effectively drop retardant. Therefore, their capabilities at indirect attack are limited. Narrow, wind-driven fires can be successfully attacked indirectly using foam drops, taking advantage of light fuels or fuel breaks. CL-215's and CL-415's are effective in supporting indirect tactics when used to reinforce retardant or other control lines, hot spotting, and knockdown of slopovers and spot fires.

j) **Supervision** – Water scoopers usually require close supervision due to frequent drops (quick turns) and working closely with ground resources. The aerial supervisor should consider the need for additional supervision in the form of another ATGS, ASM, LEAD, or HLCO as appropriate.

k) **Scooper Aircraft Communications** – Generally, communications with scooping tankers are not much different than conventional airtankers with respect to target description, clearing the line, and drop evaluations, etc.

l) **Scooping Operation** – During the scooping operation, including approach and departure from the lake, communications with the tanker should cease to allow the crew to concentrate on the pickup. The tanker will call when "up" or off the water, which will signify to the ATGS that it's okay to transmit.

m) **Foam Instructions** – Instructions can be given after the scooping operation on whether or not to inject foam and at what percent so the load has time to mix.

n) **Long Turnarounds** – On long turnarounds, request the tanker to give a one-mile final call and give your target description at that time.

o) **Standard Communications** – Confirm the line is clear, make the drop, and after the drop, evaluate the load. Instructions for the next load, including foam concentrations, can be given at this time if possible. Otherwise, wait until the tanker is "up" for the next target description.

p) **Scooper Aircraft Separation** – Once in the circuit on the fire, CL-215's and CL-415's work 500 feet AGL and lower.

    i) **Separation of Scoopers in the Circuit** – If two tankers are working the same circuit, which is very common, the aerial supervisor can choose to daisy chain the two tankers or they can be worked in tandem.

        (1) **Daisy Chaining** – One tanker is on the lake while the other drops. Generally works best for quick turn around times.

        (2) **Tandem** – One tanker leads the other. Generally works best, is more efficient, and requires less supervision for long turn around times. Also allows ground resources more time between drops to work the line.

        (3) **Four Airtankers** – If four tankers are in a circuit, they can be sequenced singly in a daisy chain, or they can be worked in two tandem pairs.

    ii) **Mixing CL-215's & CL-415's** – Both can work in the same circuit, however the CL-415's are faster and will overtake the 215's on the circuit. If possible, keep separate.

    iii) **Integrating with other Aircraft** – Scooping Tankers can be successfully integrated with suppression and logistical missions of other aircraft.

    iv) **Horizontal Separation** – The most common separation method is to assign different aircraft types to separate parts of the fire, ex., scoopers on the right flank, helicopters on the left, or conventional tankers on the left.

    v) **Sequencing** – Sequencing of aircraft can be very efficient and often is necessary but requires close supervision.

        (1) Have the scooper extend the circuit if there is a need for another aircraft to work the same area as the scooper for a short time, such as a sling load, personnel drop, or a quick recon.

(2) If another aircraft needs to work the same area as the scooper for a sustained period, either orbit the tanker or reassign.

(3) Sustained bucket operations in the same target area as scoopers is not advised, except for very long scooper turnaround times.

(4) CL-215/415 airtankers can support conventional airtankers by sequencing them in between retardant drops to cool the fire in advance of the retardant or to assist in holding the fire as it approaches the retardant.

q) **Canadian Scooper Terminology** – Following is a short list of terms relating to the use of the scooping airtankers used by Canadian Air Attack officers. Some of the terms are common to the U.S. and a few are slightly different.

i) **Fire Traffic Pattern**

(1) **Circuit:** Flight route taken by scooping airtanker from the water source to the fire and return

(a) **Typical Circuit** – Oval or rectangular flight route that is defined by an 'into the wind' pickup on the lake and a downward drop on the fire.

(b) **U-Shaped Circuit** – A flight route resembling a "U" that is defined by an 'into the wind' pickup on the lake and an 'into the wind' drop on the fire.

(c) **Figure-8 Circuit** – An intersecting flight route in the shape of an "8" that is defined by an 'into the wind' pickup on the lake and can accommodate either a crosswind drop on the head or an 'into the wind' drop elsewhere on the fire.

(d) **Base Leg** – The leg of the bombing circuit immediately preceding and perpendicular to the final leg (base leg for pickup or base leg for the drop).

(e) **Final Leg** – The last leg of the bombing circuit direct to the target or the lake.

(f) **Bomb Run** – Flight path of the tanker to the target.

ii) **Target Descriptions**

(1) **Tie-in** – Connect the drop to a specific reference point or anchor point.

(2) **Tag on** – Connect the tail end of the drop to a given point, usually the head end of the last drop.

(3) **Extend** – Tag on and lengthen the line in a specific direction.

(4) **Lap on** – Cover a previous drop entirely or to one side or the other. Reinforce.

(5) **Lap on left/right** – Cover a previous load to the left or right to widen the drop pattern, (Usually about 1/3 overlap).

(6) **Roll Up** – Connect the head end of the drop to a given point or the tail end of a previous drop.

(7) **Half On/Half Off** – Half the load on the fire, half on unburned fuel. Half & half or half in/half out.

(8) **Span** – Distance equal to one wing span of the tanker being used.

(9) **String Drop** – Trail drop

(10) **Train Drop** – Trail drop

(11) **Bull's Eye** – Load was placed exactly where requested.

(12) **Head End of Drop** – Where the last of the load hits the ground.

(13) **Tail End of Drop** – Where the load first hits the ground.

iii) **Other Terminology**

(1) **Bird Dog** – ATGS platform except Bird Dog combines low level lead-ins when deemed necessary with an orbit and direct method. Similar to the ASM.

(2) **Orbit and Direct** – Method of supervision where Bird Dog is above the fire in a right hand pattern and gives verbal targets and direction to airtankers as opposed to providing low level lead-ins.

(3) **Lead In** – Same as a lead.

(4) **Inspection Run** – Same as a low pass or dry run.

(5) **Dummy Run** – Same as a 'show me'.

(6) **Hold** – Canadians may use this term for "go around - do not drop" as well as orbit outside the incident airspace.

(7) **Stay** – May also be used to instruct a tanker to proceed to a designated location and await instruction. Hold & orbit.

(8) **Reload** – Load and return.

(9) **Period of Alert** – Duty day or duty time.

Chapter 10 - All Hazard Incidents

Introduction – Fire incidents have long utilized aerial supervision for coordinating aerial resources. The same principles of supervising and directing aircraft can also be applied to other types of incidents commonly referred to as "all hazard incidents." All hazard incidents include volcanic eruptions, earthquakes, search and rescue operations, floods, oil spills, hurricanes and spray projects.

1) Air Operations Supervision

a) **Fixed Wing and Helicopter Coordinators** – On non-fire incidents when the level or complexity of air operations exceeds the supervisory capability of the ATGS/ASM, the organization may be expanded to include a Fixed Wing Coordinator (ATCO), Helicopter Coordinator (HLCO), or both. Both positions report to the ATGS/ASM. The HLCO's role and responsibilities are basically the same as for a fire incident.

   i) The Fixed Wing Coordinator has primary responsibility for coordinating all assigned fixed wing operations at the incident. The Fixed Wing Coordinator is always airborne. More than one Fixed Wing Coordinator may be assigned to a large incident.

   ii) Large or complex incidents, which have a mix of fire and other disaster operations (earthquake or volcanic eruption), require both an ATGS/ASM and a Fixed Wing Coordinator (ATCO) to coordinate and integrate the mix of aviation assets.

b) **Criteria for Assigning Aerial Supervision** – Air operations meeting the criteria list below require a moderate to high level of supervision and coordination. Without adequate supervision and coordination air operations will very likely be less efficient, more costly and less safe. An ATGS/ASM should be assigned when an incident meets the criteria listed below.

   i) Multiple aircraft operating in incident area airspace

      (1) Mix of fixed wing and helicopter operations

      (2) Mix of low-level tactical/logistical aircraft

      (3) Periods of marginal weather, poor visibility or turbulence

   ii) Two or more branches utilizing air support

   iii) Mix of both civil and military aircraft operating in the same airspace or operations area

   iv) When conditions require airspace management, air traffic control and air resource mission priority setting and coordination

   v) Ground stations have limited ability to communicate with flying aircraft due to terrain or long distances

c) **Aerial Supervision Interaction and Communication** – The interaction between aerial supervisors (Lead, ATGS, ASM, and HLCO) is well understood and practiced on fire incidents. Interactions and communications protocol is far less established and will vary greatly on other types of incidents. Although all risk incidents retain the basic ICS organization and roles, there are incident specific technical specialist positions added to the ICS organization to supervise, coordinate and lead specific incident functions. Aerial supervisor roles may be modified to fit the incident situation and they may be coordinating directly with persons other than the traditional Operations Section Chief, Division/Group Supervisor or Strike Team/Task Force Leader. It is critical that we understand the roles and responsibilities the Technical Specialist positions, how they are identified, and how our role interacts with the Technical Specialist (chain of command, communications protocol, authority, etc.).

d) **Use of Military Aircraft** – It is important to fully understand military organization, their standard operating procedures, military aircraft capabilities and limitations, and how the ICS interfaces with military operations. An assigned Agency Aviation Military Liaison (civilian) and Military Air Operations Coordinator (civilian) will work with the Air Operations Branch Director and aerial supervisor in assigning and coordinating military air operations.

The availability of military air tactical resources may vary dramatically due to world commitments. Refer to the *Military Use Handbook (NFES 2175)* for additional information and guidance.

e) **Air Operations Associated with all Hazard Incidents** – During the past few decades, aircraft have become an important tool in combating both natural and human caused incidents. Possible uses of aircraft for various types of incidents are listed in the table below.

Table 11. Possible Uses of Aircraft by Type of Incident

Air Operations	Fire	Volcanic Eruption	Earth-quake	Search/ Rescue	Flood	Hurri-cane	Oil Spill	Spray Project	Law Enforc.
Aerial Retardant, Spray	X	X	X				X	X	
ATCO / Leadplane	X	X	X	X	X	X	X	X	
Helicopter Rappel – Personnel	X	X	X	X	X	X			X
Helicopter Land – Personnel	X	X	X	X	X	X	X	X	X
Parachute Delivery – Personnel	X	X	X	X	X	X	X		
Parachute Delivery – Cargo	X	X	X	X	X	X	X		
Helicopter Sling Load – Cargo	X	X	X	X	X	X	X		X
Helicopter Internal – Cargo	X	X	X	X	X	X	X	X	X
Recon/Assessment – Fixed Wing	X	X	X	X	X	X	X	X	X
Recon/Assessment – Helicopter	X	X	X	X	X	X	X	X	X
Search – Fixed Wing	X	X	X	X	X	X			X
Search – Helicopter	X	X	X	X	X	X			X
Medevac – Helicopter	X	X	X	X	X	X	X	X	X
Medevac – Short Haul Heli.	X	X	X	X	X	X	X	X	X
IR Detect/Map - Fixed Wing	X	X	X		X		X		X
IR Detect/Map – Helicopter	X	X			X		X		X
Helitorch	X						X		
ATGS or Air Traffic Control	X	X	X	X	X	X	X	X	X
News Media	X	X	X	X	X	X	X	X	X
VIP Flights	X	X	X	X	X	X	X	X	X

This page intentionally left blank.

Chapter 11 – Safety

Safety is the principal consideration in all aspects of aerial supervision. A safe aviation operation depends on accurate risk assessment and informed decision making.

Risk levels are established by the severity of possible events and the probability that they will occur. Assessing risk identifies the hazard, the associated risk, and places the hazard in a relationship to the mission. A decision to conduct a mission requires weighing the risk against the benefit of the mission and deciding whether the risks are acceptable. Examples of the Risk Management Process are available in the *Incident Response Pocket Guide* (IRPG), the *Interagency Standards for Fire and Fire Aviation Operations* (Red Book), CALFIRE 8300, and the *Interagency Helicopter Operations Guide* (IHOG).

Factors to consider during the risk assessment process:

1) Any flight mission has a degree of risk that varies from 0% (no flight activity is conducted) to 100% (aircraft and/or personnel experience a mishap).
2) The aerial supervisor must identify hazards, analyze the degree of risk associated with each, and place hazards in perspective relative to the mission or task
3) Hazards might not always be limited to the performance of flight, but may include hazards to personnel if the flight is not performed.
4) The risk assessment may include the aerial supervisor, Air Operations Branch Director, Duty Officers, agency Fire Management Staff, Incident Commanders, Dispatchers, and Line Officers/Managers.
5) **Ultimately the pilot in command has the authority to decline a flight mission that he or she considers excessively hazardous.**

1) Mitigating Risks

In some cases the aerial supervisor may have to shut down air operations. Air operations **must not** proceed until risk mitigation measures are implemented. Risk mitigation measures to consider:

Risk Mitigation Considerations

a) **Monitor the overall aviation operation for human factors related issues**

    i) Task saturation

    ii) Fatigue, burnout, and stress

    iii) Acceptance of risk as normal

    iv) Lack of situational awareness

b) **Monitor effectiveness of the overall air operation**

    i) Ensure suppression objectives are truly obtainable

        (1) Risk versus reward – Is the mission worth it?

        (2) Is there adequate ground support?

        (3) Are there adequate aerial resources?

ii)   Is there enough time in the operational period?

iii)   Monitor weather conditions for increasing winds, turbulence, thunderstorms, or decreasing visibility.

iv)   Be proactive in communicating current fire and fire weather conditions.

v)   Provide realistic input regarding resource needs commensurate with successful completion/modification of incident objectives.

c)   **Utilize the appropriate aircraft for the mission**

     i)   Turbine vs. piston

     ii)   Heavy tankers vs. SEATs

     iii)   Density altitude issues

     iv)   Helicopter types

d)   **Communications Planning** – When discreet radio frequencies are used during incident operations, ensure contact frequencies such as command and air to ground are monitored by appropriate ground personnel. Make sure that ground personnel know how to reach the aerial supervision resources.

e)   **Order Additional Frequencies** – Order additional frequencies as needed for operations; as incident complexities increase, the aerial supervisor must ensure adequate radio frequency coverage. Be proactive. There can be up to a 24-hour delay from the time a frequency is ordered to the time it is assigned to the incident.

f)   **Establish Positive Air Traffic Control** – Hold aircraft in the air or on the ground until structured traffic patterns can be established.

g)   **Limit Number of Airborne Aircraft** – Limit number of aircraft working an incident per visibility, routing procedures and communications capability.

h)   **Obtain Input** – Discuss operations safety with Leadplane, Helicopter Coordinator and contract pilots. Mission debriefings are an excellent source of information; **Air crewmembers will utilize After Action Reviews (AAR) to critique mission effectiveness with other incident and airbase personnel as often as possible.**

i)   **System Safety Assessment** – The effectiveness of risk assessment and management can be increased through utilization of the current System Safety Assessment for Aerial Supervision Operations.

The following assessment of aerial supervision operations has been developed for aerial supervisors. It identifies hazards, the likelihood of encountering them and the risk associated with exposure to the hazard. Mitigations are listed for each hazard as well as the post mitigation risk.

System Safety utilization is standard operating procedure and covers all aspects of aerial supervision. It should be used for incident operations, training and review by agency air crewmembers.

Table 12. System Safety Assessment for Aerial Supervision

System - Aircraft

Sub-systems	Hazards	Pre Mitigation Likelihood	Pre Mitigation Severity	Pre Mitigation Outcome	Mitigation	Post mitigation Likelihood	Post mitigation Severity	Post mitigation Outcome
Avionics	Avionics failure.	Occasional	Marginal	Medium	Minimum equipment list (MEL) establishes minimum requirement. Mission requirements as determined by the flight crew. Integrate into preflight checklist.	Improbable	Negligible	Low
	Avionics package insufficient for mission complexity.	Probable	Critical	High	Contract specifications that recognize mission requirements. Ensure necessary type, configuration, and number of radios to complete mission safely. Reduce span of control. Limit operations.	Remote	Marginal	Medium
	Contract pilot unfamiliar with avionics. (Can't run radios or GPS, etc.).	Occasional	Marginal	Medium	Release, replace the pilot, Enforce contract specifications.	Remote	Negligible	Low
Aircraft Type	Reduced field of view for the flight crew.	Occasional	Critical	Serious	Ensure aircraft is appropriate for the mission. Flight profile altered to maximize visibility. Use of TCAS. Clear communication with other aircraft. Alter interior configuration (headrest, seat, windows).	Improbable	Negligible	Low
Performance Standards	Poor Engine performance (single/twin, turbine/recip) for the ATGS mission	Occasional	Catastrophic	High	Plan for high density altitudes. Download cargo/fuel load. Relocate to favorable location. Alter the mission. Upgrade the aircraft. Ensure aircraft is appropriate for the mission. Perform pre-flight planning.	Remote	Catastrophic	Serious
Contracting	Contract pilot skill/fire experience leading to sub-standard performance (i.e. working avionics, flight skills) during flight operations.	Remote	Critical	Medium	Thorough briefing. Ride along with veteran fire pilot. Use contract evaluation process. Contractor training. Computer based training. Give air attack pilots a check ride every three years.	Improbable	Critical	Medium
Fuel	Capacity and Procedure, ground fueling errors.	Frequent	Catastrophic	High	Verify adequate volume of fuel for mission. Ensure proper fueling procedures are followed for type of aircraft.	Remote	Critical	Medium

System - Flight Operations

Sub-systems	Hazards	Pre Mitigation Likelihood	Pre Mitigation Severity	Pre Mitigation Outcome	Mitigation	Post mitigation Likelihood	Post mitigation Severity	Post mitigation Outcome
	Restricted visibility.	Frequent	Catastrophic	High	Limit exposure. Determine effectiveness of the operation (risk vs. benefit) and discontinue if warranted. Limit number of aircraft in operating area. Increase vertical/horizontal separation of aircraft.	Occasional	Critical	Serious
	Wake turbulence.	Occasional	Critical	Serious	Situational awareness assists prevention. Communication helps to avoid wake turbulence areas. Wake turbulence avoidance procedures (altitude, time, distance)	Remote	Critical	Medium
	Weather (Turbulence/wind/T-storms).	Frequent	Critical	High	Adjust tactics or shut down air ops. Increase vertical/horizontal separation of aircraft. Utilize human aided technology (weather radar, etc.). Encourage dispatch to obtain/communicate weather information. Utilize and share pilot reports of severe weather.	Occasional	Critical	Serious
Mission	Poor fuel management.	Occasional	Critical	Serious	Monitor fuel quantities. Follow fuel transfer procedures.	Remote	Critical	Medium
	Controlled Flight Into Terrain (CFIT) due to low level operations.	Frequent	Catastrophic	High	Ensure high level recon is completed prior to commencing low level flight. Manage radio communication. Proper aircraft configuration. Reduce exposure time in low level. Consult sectional chart/hazard map, Consult ground personnel/other AC. Obtain local knowledge. Utilize local knowledge.	Remote	Catastrophic	Serious
	Operating in close proximity to other aircraft (collision potential)	Frequent	Catastrophic	High	Communication established with all aircraft. Situational awareness. TCAS Establish clear and concise directions for simultaneous operations, (virtual fence, geographic separation, altitude separation, holding/timing, Establish Initial point, ingress/egress route.	Remote	Catastrophic	Serious

Sub-systems	Hazards	Pre Mitigation Likelihood	Pre Mitigation Severity	Pre Mitigation Outcome	Mitigation	Post mitigation Likelihood	Post mitigation Severity	Post mitigation Outcome
Mission	Reliance on technology causes distraction, low situational awareness, division of attention in the cockpit.	Frequent	Catastrophic	High	Maintain situation awareness. Maintain see and avoid techniques Prioritize mission/cockpit workload. Utilize CRM practices.	Remote	Catastrophic	Serious
	Aircraft emergency (engine out, fire, bird strike, mechanical failure, etc.).	Occasional	Catastrophic	High	Crew cross training and familiarization with a/c systems and emergency procedure checklists (pinch hitter/simulator training).	Remote	Catastrophic	Serious
	Exceeded span of control.	Occasional	Critical	Serious	Ensure roles and responsibilities are assigned and understood within aerial supervision crew. Assign aircraft to common functions and tasks with a single point of contact. Hold aircraft at base to limit the number of assigned aircraft over the incident.	Remote	Critical	Medium
	Unclear objectives / tactics.	Frequent	Critical	High	Ensure strategy and tactics are clear and understood. Use common terminology, solicit/utilize feedback.	Occasional	Critical	Serious
	ATGS performance results in hazardous operation.	Occasional	Critical	Serious	Shut down the operation, Deconflict the area. Return to base to rebrief the mission. Mentor, proficiency checkride, retrain / recertify.	Remote	Critical	Medium
	Unnecessary exposure due to inefficient operational use of tactical aircraft.	Probable	Critical	High	SOPs for all tactical aircraft types. Right tool for job. Training, feedback, brief/debrief.	Remote	Critical	Medium
Airspace	FTA: Aircraft not complying with procedures.	Probable	Catastrophic	High	Aerial supervision enforces FTA procedures.	Improbable	Critical	Medium
	Multiple initial attack incidents in same area cause confusion; near miss hazard.	Probable	Critical	High	Coordinate with dispatch and other aircraft. Ensure fire names, frequencies, locations, and aircraft assignments are communicated to all flight crews.	Probable	Critical	Serious
	Special use airspace: Aircraft not having authorization to enter the SUA, not coordinating with controlling agency.	Probable	Critical	High	See and avoid. Know SUA areas. Establish communication with controlling agency. Thorough briefings.	Remote	Critical	Medium
	Non-incident aircraft intrusion in TFR.	Probable	Catastrophic	High	See and avoid, Inform other aircraft on scene. Reevaluate TFR promotion.	Remote	Catastrophic	Serious

Sub-systems	Hazards	Pre Mitigation Likelihood	Pre Mitigation Severity	Pre Mitigation Outcome	Mitigation	Post mitigation Likelihood	Post mitigation Severity	Post mitigation Outcome
Airspace	Fires in proximity to airport/airstrip. Potential for mid-air collision or intrusion in FTA.	Occasional	Catastrophic	High	Implement/Validate TFR as incident expands, Deconflict SUA, Establish communication with controlling agency, Notify other aircraft. Provide TFR transition corridors for non-incident aircraft on large incidents. Increase awareness of GA operators and other agency flight crews not assigned to incident.	Remote	Catastrophic	Serious
	Radio frequency congestion.	Frequent	Critical	High	Exercise radio discipline/order additional frequencies as needed.	Remote	Critical	Medium
	State/County/Rural resources on different bandwidth.	Probable	Critical	High	Coordinate with cooperators to find a way to communicate with one another.	Remote	Critical	Medium
Communications	Hazardous air operations resulting from inaccurate information disseminated through the dispatch system.	Frequent	Critical	High	Verify information at time of dispatch. Flight crews will brief/debrief with dispatchers. Provide aviation training for dispatchers. Maintain qualified dispatcher on the A/C desk.	Occasional	Critical	Serious

System - Personnel

Sub-systems	Hazards	Pre Mitigation Likelihood	Pre Mitigation Severity	Pre Mitigation Outcome	Mitigation	Post mitigation Likelihood	Post mitigation Severity	Post mitigation Outcome
Human Factors	Loss of situational awareness due to aircrew fatigue/burnout.	Probable	Critical	High	Adhere to flight and duty limitations policy. Activate phase limitations.	Occasional	Critical	Serious
	Hazardous air operations developing through ineffective CRM.	Remote	Critical	Medium	Re-evaluate task allocation. Brief and debrief.	Improbable	Critical	Medium
	Acceptance of high risk as normal. (Complacency).	Probable	Catastrophic	High	Reevaluate risk vs. benefit. Solicit feedback from other flight crews. Utilize CRM to validate mission parameters. Validate mission, or remove the high risk taking individual from the mission.	Remote	Catastrophic	Serious
	Hazardous air operations developing due to external pressures.	Occasional	Critical	Serious	Do not allow external pressure to influence the operation. Utilize CRM to ensure an effective operation with acceptable level of risk.	Remote	Critical	Medium
	Hazardous attitude: Anti authority, macho, invulnerability, impulsiveness, and resignation.	Frequent	Critical	High	Remove the individual from the mission. Properly supervise employees. Adhere to work-rest guidelines, flight and duty limitations policy, etc. Validate and stick to incident strategy and tactics.	Occasional	Critical	Serious

2) Modifying Air Operations

There is no way to define an exact trigger point for adjusting, downsizing, or completely suspending aviation operations. The factors listed below should be evaluated to determine whether additional aerial supervision resources are needed or tactical/logistical missions need to be modified/suspended:

a) Complexity of aviation operations

b) Communications

c) Topography (fire size, position on slope, location, etc.)

d) Firefighter and public safety

e) Poor visibility

f) Wind

g) Turbulence

h) Fire behavior

i) ATGS Fire Orders & Watch out Situation (see below)

j) Aircraft incident/accident

k) Aircraft/Aircrew performance

3) Aerial Supervision Fire Orders

In addition to the 10 Standard Fire Orders and 18 Watch Out Situations, the aerial supervision community has developed similar memory aids for air crews. The following orders apply to those who supervise and coordinate air tactical operations. These orders highlight the most critical responsibilities and concerns of aerial supervisors. Adherence to these orders will help achieve an effective and safe air operation.

A: Assign air resources based on fire size-up, hazard assessment, resource capability and the tactical plan.

T: Terminate operations that are unsafe or ineffective.

G: Guarantee flight safety by practicing good radio frequency management and airspace management.

S: Strictly adhere to and enforce agency policies, FAR's and standard operating procedures.

F: Fight fire aggressively but provide for safe ground and air operations.

I: Inform Operations when tactics are completed, ineffective or unsafe - advise on options.

R: Recognize and alert ground personnel of fire conditions and air missions which may jeopardize ground safety. (You are their eyes in the sky).

E: Ensure instructions are clear, accurate and expressed in standard terms.

O: Organize air tactical operations to provide continuous air tactical supervision.

R: Require communications be maintained with ground operations and assigned air resources.

D: Determine and assign safe flight routes and patterns with adequate vertical and horizontal separation.

E: Establish procedures to achieve coordination, aircraft separation and flight safety.

R: Remain in control of all air resources at all times.

S: Stay alert, keep calm, think clearly and act decisively.

4) Aerial Supervision Watch Out Situations

When one or more of the following situations exists, air operations safety and effectiveness are in jeopardy. Address the situation(s) before continuing operations.

a) Fire is not thoroughly scouted for aviation safety hazards

b) Fire has not been thoroughly sized up and a strategic/tactical plan has not been developed

c) Air resources do not clearly understand location of mission target area and their tactical objectives

d) Air resources are not aware of all flight hazards

e) Flight routes and altitude assignments have not been established, identified and communicated

f) Visibility is poor and air resources have difficulty seeing ground hazards and maintaining visual contact with other air resources

g) Poor or intermittent communications with ground operations and other air resources

h) Ground resources are not continuously monitoring and communicating on the tactical Ground-to-Air frequency

i) Wind, turbulence and visibility make missions ineffective or unsafe

j) Simultaneous arrival of air resources working in the same airspace without establishing mission priorities and coordination

k)   Radio frequency overload or inattention makes communication difficult or ineffective

l)   Aircraft are in the incident airspace with inoperable radio(s)

m)   There is an airspace intrusion by a non-incident aircraft

n)   MOA's or MTR's have not been deactivated

o)   A TFR has not been imposed or its dimensions do not include all operations areas

p)   Operations in congested airspace/areas without a Leadplane

q)   Incident is located on, or near flight routes to airports

r)   Aircraft are making altitude changes without prior clearance

s)   Aircraft enter the incident airspace without proper clearance

t)   Air tactics supervision is interrupted by need for fuel or relief or an emergency

u)   Roll clouds

v)   Blowing dust

w)   Helicopters using buckets must cross interstate highways or cross sub-divisions in order to reload with suppressant/retardant

x)   Simultaneous transitions between ATGS, Lead, or ASM

Chapter 12 – Job Aids and Resources

1) Required Job Aids (Lead/ASM)

Full U.S. (Contiguous United States) approach and low altitude en route IFR chart coverage.

2) Aerial Supervision Kit

Each aerial supervisor should have and maintain a kit. The following items are recommended to be on board the aircraft:

a) **Knee Board** – Leg board/clip board.

b) **Headset**

c) **Frequency Guide**

d) **Batteries** – Headset, Camera, flashlight, etc.

e) **Flashlight**

f) **Camera**

g) **Overnight Bag**

h) **Maps**

    i) Current FAA sectional chart coverage area

    ii) Agency Maps

    iii) Retardant Base Coverage Map

    iv) Local Hazard Map (from Airtanker Base Manager or Dispatch)

    v) Incident Map (updated daily)

    vi) Retardant base map

i) **Air Tactical Forms** – Download from the NIFC aviation Web page at: http://www.blm.gov/nifc/st/en/prog/fire/Aviation/aerial_supervision.html

    i) Fire Sizeup

    ii) ATGS/Lead/ASM checkride

    iii) Initial Attack/Extended Attack ATGS Form

    iv) SEAT Pilot Mission Documentation Log

    v) Aerial Supervision Transition Checklist

    vi) Leadplane, ASM, or ATGS Mission Log

    vii) Airtanker Briefing Checklist

    viii) Aerial Supervision Cost Summary

    ix) Pilot Flight time and Duty Day Tracking

3) Publications

a) *Interagency Smokejumper Pilot Operations Guide*

b) *Interagency Smokejumper Operations Guide*

c) *Interagency Standards for Fire and Fire Aviation Operations* (Red Book), NFES 2724

d) Tables of sunrise and sunset

e) Radio frequency guide

f) FS-5700-1 Visual Signal Code Card

g) Radio programming directions

h) Recommended retardant coverage levels

i) Airtanker line length production charts

j) Agency specific information and policies

k) Incident Action Plan (IAP): Available daily through ATGS, Air Operations Branch Director or Dispatch

l) Aviation Safety Communiqué (SAFECOM): FS-5700-14 and OAS-34

m) *Interagency Air Space Coordination Guide*

n) *National Interagency Mobilization Guide*, NFES 2092

o) Geographic (agency) mobilization guide

p) Forest (unit) mobilization guide

q) Agency aviation management manual handbooks

r) USDI - USDA aircraft radio communications and frequency guide

s) National airtanker contract

t) Airtanker base operations guide and directory

u) Agency aviation plan

v) Area Planning AP/1B Chart (military training routes)

w) *Military Use Handbook*, NFES 2175

x) *Interagency Single Engine Airtanker Operations Guide* (ISOG), PMS 506.

y) *Interagency Helicopter Operations Guide* (IHOG), PMS 510.

z) *Interagency Aviation Mishap Response Guide and Checklist*, PMS 503.

Glossary

Term	Description
Abeam	An aircraft is abeam a fix, point, or object when the fix/point/object is approximately 90 degrees left or right of the aircrafts track
Abort	To terminate a planned aircraft maneuver
Action Plan	Any tactical plan developed by any element of ICS in support of the incident action plan
AGL	Above ground level
AIR Attack	ICS identifier for the Air Tactical Group Supervisor
Airtanker Coordinator (ATCO)	Airborne position supervised by the Air Tactical Group Supervisor. Assigns airtankers to specific targets. Supervises and evaluates drops. The position is normally filled with a Leadplane.
"A" (Alpha)	Designation for State of Alaska DNR ASM Aircraft.
Anchor Point	A strategic and safe point or area, usually a barrier to fire spread, from which to start construction of the control line.
ASM	Federal designation for an Aerial Supervision Module platform with an Air Tactical Pilot and Air Tactical Supervisor on board. This module can perform aerial supervision and low-level operations including the lead profile.
Assigned to	Tactical resource allocated to an incident. The resource may be flying en route to and from, or on hold at a ground site
ATP	Federally designated Air Tactical Pilot. Pilot of an ASM who is primarily responsible for aircraft safety and providing aircraft coordination over the incident. The ATP meets the Interagency training requirements for Leadplane operations and has completed ASM/CRM training.
ATS	The ATS is a qualified ATGS who has received specialized training and authorization to function as an ASM crewmember. The ATS is an ATGS who also utilizes CRM to evaluate and share the incident workload with the ATP.

Term	Description
Backfire	Fire set between the control line and the main fire to consume unburned materials to stop the advance of the main fire. A backfire is only used when the main fire is burning actively enough to suck the backfire against the wind.
Barrier	Any obstruction to the spread of the fire. Typically an area or strip devoid of flammable fuel.
Blowup	Sudden increase in fire intensity or rate of spread sufficient to preclude direct control.
Base (of a fire)	The part of the fire perimeter opposite the head (see origin). Also referred to as rear or heel.
"B" BRAVO	Federal designation for Aerial Supervision Modules.
Break (left or right)	Means turn left or right. Applies to aircraft in flight, usually on the drop run and when given as a command to the pilot. Implies immediate compliance.
Burn out	Fire set at the inside edge of a control line to consume unburned materials between the fire and the control line. Usually associated with indirect attack.
Canopy	The stratum containing the crowns of the tallest vegetation present (living or dead), usually above 20 feet
Cardinal Points	The four chief points of the compass: North, South, East, and West.
Civil Twilight	Civil Twilight is defined to begin in the morning, and to end in the evening when the center of the Sun is geometrically 6 degrees below the horizon. This is the limit at which twilight illumination is sufficient, under good weather conditions, for terrestrial objects to be clearly distinguished.
Clock Method	A means of establishing a target or point by reference to clock directions where the nose of the aircraft is 12 o' clock, moving clockwise to the right wing at 3 o'clock, the tail at 6 o'clock, and the left wing at 9 o'clock.

Term	Description
Configuration	How the aircraft is equipped, outfitted, modified for a mission or segment of a mission. Also refers to use of drag devices (flaps, gear) to modify flight characteristics.
Congested Area	FAA (non-specific) term for areas that require additional precautions and procedures to conduct low-level flight operations. It is applied by the FAA on a case-by-case basis. The regulation addresses, "any congested area of a city, town, or settlement, or over any open air assembly of persons...."
Constant Flow Tank	A single compartment with two doors controlled by a computer. Capable of single or multiple even flow drops at designated coverage levels from .5 GPC to 8 GPC
Control Line	An inclusive term for all constructed or natural fire barriers and treated fire edge used to control a fire's spread.
Cover Assignment	Airtankers ordered to a different base to provide initial attack coverage at the new base. Sometimes referred to as "Move Up and Cover."
Coverage Level	A numerical value representing the number of gallons of retardant mixture dropped, or prescribed, to cover fuels in a 100 sq. ft. area (GPC).
Cut Off Time	Time when operations involving low level flight maneuvers must be suspended.
Delayed Attack Fire	A fire that, due to its lower priority and/or unavailability of ground resources, will not be staffed for several hours or possibly several days.
Direct Attack	Control effort (retardant line, fireline) conducted at fire perimeter (fire edge) - usually under low fire intensity conditions.
Divert	Change in aircraft assignment from one target to another or to a new incident.
Drift Correction	Offset flight path flown to compensate for wind induced retardant drift.

Term	Description
Drift Smoke	Smoke that has drifted from its point of origin and has lost any original billow form.
Drop	Aerial release of paracargo, retardant, or water/foam.
Drop Configuration	The type of drop the pilot selects to achieve the desired coverage level based on the aircrafts door/tank system.
Drop Zone	The area around the target to be dropped on.
Dry Run	A low pass over the target without dropping to evaluate drop conditions and/or alert ground personnel of an impending live run.
Early	Indicating drop was early or short of the target.
Engine	(In fire context) A ground vehicle crewed by firefighters that dispenses water or foam normally with fire hoses and nozzles.
Escape Route	The safest, quickest or most direct route between a firefighter's location and a safety zone.
Exit	Term used to indicate the flight route away from the drop area.
Extend/Tag on	Drop retardant so that the load overlaps and lengthens a previous drop.
False Alarm	A reported smoke or fire requiring no suppression action.
Finger	A narrow elongated portion of a fire projecting from the main body.
Fire Break	A natural or constructed barrier used to stop or check fires or to provide a control line from which to work.
Fireline	A control line that is void of burnable material. Fire lines are normally constructed by hand crews.
Fire Perimeter	The active burning edge of a fire or its exterior burned limits.

Term	Description
Fire Shelter	An aluminized, heat reflective, firefighters personal protective pup tent used in fire entrapment situations. The heat reflection capability of the exterior is the primary function of the shelter. DO NOT drop fire retardants on the tent, as it will compromise the heat reflection capability of the shelter.
Fixed Tank	A tank mounted inside or directly underneath an aircraft, which contains water or retardant for dropping on a fire.
Fixed Wing Coordinator	A non-fire airborne position designed to supervise airplanes on incidents.
Flanking Attack	An attack made along the flanks of a fire either simultaneously or successively from a less active or anchor point and endeavoring to connect the two lines to the head.
Flanks	The parts of a fire perimeter that are roughly parallel to the main direction of spread. The left flank is the left side as viewed from the base of the fire, looking toward the head.
FLIR	Forward Looking Infrared
FLIR/ATGS	ATGS aircraft equipped with FLIR. FLIR used in ATGS operations.
FM	Refer to VHF-FM
Fuel Break	A wide strip or block of land on which the vegetation has been permanently modified to a low volume fuel type so that fires burning into it can be more readily controlled.
Fugitive Retardant	A clear retardant, without iron oxide (red color agent), or a retardant with a red color agent that fades or becomes invisible after several days exposure to ultraviolet sunrays.
Gap	A weak or missed area in a retardant line.
Go Around	Abort the retardant run.
Gel	Water, which is chemically enhanced and utilizes in direct attack operations as a suppressant.

Term	Description
GPC	A term relating to retardant coverage levels meaning Gallons per 100 Sq. Ft.
Head	The most rapidly spreading portion of a fire perimeter, normally located on the leeward or up slope side.
HEL CO (HLCO)	Call sign identifier of the Helicopter Coordinator
Here	Term communicated by the Leadplane pilot to the airtanker or helitanker pilot identifying the target location and starting point of a drop.
Helitanker	Heavy (Type 1) Helicopters configured with fixed tanks or a bucket for dropping water, foam, or retardant.
Hold (Holding Area)	A predetermined flight pattern, which keeps aircraft within a specified airspace while awaiting further clearance.
Holding Action	Use of an aerial application to reduce fire intensity and fire spread until ground resources arrive. Common with delayed attack fires.
Hoselay	Arrangement of connected lengths of fire hose and accessories beginning at the first pumping unit and ending at the point of water delivery.
Hotshot Crew	A highly trained firefighting crew used primarily in hand line construction.
Hotspot	A particularly active part of a fire.
Indirect Attack	Control line located along natural or human made firebreaks, favorable breaks in topography or at a considerable distance from the fire perimeter.
Initial Point (IP)	A reporting location clearly identified by the aerial supervisor. It may be a lat/long or geographic point (landmark).

Term	Description
Intervalometer	A cockpit mounted electronic device/selector box which actuates the compartment door singly or multiple doors simultaneously or in sequence, at preset time intervals. Pilot or co-pilot selects number of doors and time interval between doors to produce the desired coverage level and line length.
Island	Green or unburned area within the fire perimeter.
Jettison	To dispose of (drop) unused retardant prior to landing.
Knock Down	To reduce flame or heat in a specified target. Indicates the retardant load should fall directly on the burning perimeter or object. Used to assist ground forces.
Late	Indicating the drop was late or overshot the target.
Leadplane	An airplane crewed by a qualified Leadplane pilot tasked to lead airtankers in low-level drop runs.
Leadplane Pilot	Performs Airtanker Coordinator duties and is authorized to conduct flights below 500 feet AGL to access flight conditions, hazards, and to identify the target.
Leadplane Check Pilot	A Leadplane pilot designated by the USDA-FS or BLM to evaluate Leadplane pilot trainees for initial certification and Leadplane pilots for recertification.
Leadplane Pilot Instructor (LPI)	Leadplane pilot designated by the USDA-FS or BLM to train Leadplane pilot trainees.
Live Run	A flight over the drop area in which a discharge of cargo or retardant/water will be made.
Load and Hold	The airtanker is being ordered to reload and hold at the retardant base awaiting further instructions.
Load and Return	The airtanker is being ordered to reload and return to the fire with the load of retardant.
Low Pass	Low altitude run over the target area used by the Leadplane pilot and/or airtanker pilots to identify the target and assess flight conditions on the approach and exit.

Term	Description
MAFFS	Modular Airborne Firefighting Systems - Military aircraft equipped to drop retardant. Used in emergencies to supplement commercial airtankers.
Main Ridge	Prominent ridge line separating river or creek drainage. Usually has numerous smaller ridges (spur ridges) extending outward from both sides. Can be confusing if not covered in orientation.
Mayday	International distress signal/call. When repeated three times it indicates imminent and grave danger and that immediate assistance is required.
Leadplane Pilot Mentor	A pilot with a minimum of 2 years experience as a qualified Leadplane pilot assigned to assist a trainee Leadplane pilot to successfully complete training.
Mission (Leadplane)	A Leadplane mission consists of a flight on an actual fire where retardant is dropped. Each additional fire flown during a single flight counts as an additional mission.
Mission (ATGS)	An ATGS mission consists of a flight on an actual incident where coordination of airborne resources takes place. Each additional incident flown during a single flight counts as an additional mission.
MOA	A Military Operations Area (Special Use Area) found on aeronautical sectional charts.
MSL	Mean Sea Level.
MTR	A Military Training Route found on aeronautical sectional chart and AP/1B maps. Routes accommodate low-altitude training operations - below 10,000ft. MSL - in excess of 250 KIAS.
On Target	Acknowledgment to pilot that the drop was well placed.
Orbit	see Hold
Origin	Point on the ground where the fire first started.
Overrun (Overtake)	Unintentional passing of the aircraft in the lead by the trailing aircraft.

Term	Description
Parallel Attack	A control effort generally parallel to the fire perimeter, usually several feet to +100 ft. away. Allows line construction before the fires lateral spread outflanks line construction operations.
Perimeter	The outside edge of the fire.
Pockets	Areas of unburned fuel along the fire perimeter.
Portion of Load	Portion of the airtanker retardant to be dropped. Portions are identified by fractions of the load (1/4, 1/3, ½), whole load, or defined start/stop points on the ground.
Pre Treat	Laying retardant line in advance of the fire where ground cover or terrain is best for fire control action, or to reinforce a control line, often used in indirect attack.
Reburn	Subsequent burning of an area in which fire has previously burned but has left flammable fuel that ignites when burning conditions are more favorable.
Retardant (Long Term)	Contains a chemical that alters the combustion process and causes cooling, smothering, or insulating of fuels. Remains effective until diluted or rinsed off.
Retardant (Short Term)	Chemical mixture whose effectiveness relies mostly on its ability to retain moisture, thereby cooling the fire. Common short-term retardants are water and foam.
Rotor Span	The length of a rotor diameter. Used to make adjustments in alignment of flight route when dropping water/retardant.
Route (Flight)	The path an aircraft takes from the point of departure to the destination.
Running	Behavior of a fire, or portion of a fire, spreading rapidly with a well-defined head.
Saddle	Depression or pass in a ridge line.

Term	Description
Safety Zone	An area used for escape in the event the fireline is overrun or outflanked, or in case a spot fire causes fuels outside the control line to render the fireline unsafe. During an emergency, airtankers may be asked to re-enforce a safety zone using retardant drops.
Scratch Line	A preliminary control line hastily built with hand tools as an emergency measure to check the spread of a fire.
Secondary Line	A fireline built some distance away from the primary control line, used as a backup against slopovers and spot fires.
Shoulder	The part of the fire where the flank joins the head. Referred to as left or right shoulder.
Slash	Debris left after logging, pruning, thinning or brush cutting.
Slopover	The extension of a fire across a control line.
Smoldering	Behavior of a fire burning without flame and slowly spreading.
Snag	A standing, dead (defoliated) tree. Often called stub, if less than 20 feet tall.
Special Use Mission (DOI)	Flight operations requiring special pilot skills/experience and aircraft equipment to perform the mission.
Spot Fire	A fire caused by the transfer of burning material through the air into flammable material beyond the perimeter of the main fire.
Spotting	Behavior of a fire producing sparks or embers that are carried by the wind and start new fires outside the perimeter of the main fire.
Spur ridge	A small ridge, which extends finger-like from a main ridge.
Strategy	The general plan or direction selected to accomplish incident objectives (i.e.: direct, indirect, or parallel attack).
SUA	Special Use Airspace including Military Operations Areas (MOA's), Restricted Areas, Prohibited Areas, Alert Areas, Warning Areas, and Controlled Firing Areas.

Term	Description
Suppressant	A water or chemical solution that is applied directly to burning fuels. Intended to extinguish rather than retard.
Surface Fire	Fire that burns surface litter, other loose debris of the forest floor, and small vegetation.
Tactic	Deploying and directing resources to accomplish the objectives designated by the strategy (i.e.: hoselay, handline, retardant line, or wet line).
Target	The area or object you want a retardant /water drop to cover.
TCAS	Traffic Collision Avoidance System, electronic aid that gives the azimuth, distance, and relative altitude of transponder-equipped aircraft in relation to the TCAS equipped aircraft.
TFR (91.137)	Temporary Flight Restriction. Airspace within which certain flight restrictions apply.
Tie In	To connect a retardant drop with a specified point (road, stream, previous drop, etc.).
Traffic Pattern	The recommended flight path for aircraft arriving at and departing from an airport.
Traffic Pattern- Base	A flight path at right angles to the landing runway or target off its approach end.
Traffic Pattern- Crosswind	A flight path at the right angles to the landing runway or target off its upwind end.
Traffic Pattern - Downwind	A flight path parallel to the landing runway or target in a direction opposite to landing or drop direction.
Traffic Pattern - Final	A flight path in the direction of, and prior to, the landing or drop area.
Traffic Pattern - Upwind	A flight path parallel to the direction of the final before turning crosswind.

Term	Description
UHF	Ultra High Frequency. Common to military aircraft. Incompatible with VHF radio system. Operates in 300-3000 MHz range.
VHF	Very high frequency radio. The standard aircraft radio that all civil and most military aircraft use to communicate with FAA facilities and other aircraft.
VHF-AM	Amplitude modulation - Aircraft radio - ranges 118 MHz to 136.975 MHz. Used on wildland fire incidents for ground-to-air and air-to-air communications.
VHF-FM	Frequency modulation radio, multi-agency radio commonly used for dispatch, land-based mobile and airborne communications. Operates in range of 138 MHz to 174 MHz.
Variable Flow Tank System	Multiple tanks or compartments controlled by an electronic intervalometer control mechanism to open doors singly, simultaneously or multiple doors in an interval sequence.
Victor	Another way of referring to VHF-AM.
Virtual Fence	Landmark or feature utilized to maintain horizontal aircraft separation.
Waterway	Any body of water including lakes, rivers, streams, and ponds whether or not they contain aquatic life.
Wingspan	The length of the airtankers wing span from tip to tip. Used to make low level ground track adjustments. Note: Adjustments less than half a wingspan are given in feet.

Abbreviations

Abbreviation	Description
AFMC	Air Force Mission Commander
ASM	Aerial Supervision Module
AFS	Alaska Fire Service
AMIS	Aviation Management Information System
ATCO	Airtanker Coordinator (Leadplane)
ATF	Aerial Task Force
ATGS	Air Tactical Group Supervisor
BIA	Bureau of Indian Affairs
BLM	Bureau of Land Management
CDF	California Department of Forestry
CO	Contracting Officer
COR	Contracting Officers Representative
CWN	Call When Needed
DM	Departmental Manual (DOI)
DOI	Department of the Interior (Also written as USDI)
ECC	Emergency Communication Center
FMP	Fire Management Plan
FSM	Forest Service Manual
FSH	Forest Service Handbook
GACC	Geographic Area Coordination Center
GPC	Gallons per 100 Sq. Feet (Retardant)
HIGE	Hover In Ground Effect
HLCO	Helicopter Coordinator
ICS	Incident Command System
IP	Initial Point
LPI	Leadplane Pilot Instructor
MABM	MAFFS Airtanker Base Manager
MAFFS	Modular Airborne Fire Fighting System

Abbreviation	Description
MLO	Military Liaison Officer / MAFFS Liaison Officer
MOU	Memorandum of Understanding
NAO	National Aviation Office (BLM and USFS)
NAOO	National Aviation Operations Officer (USFS.)
NICC	National Interagency Coordination Center
NIFC	National Interagency Fire Center
NPS	National Park Service
NWCG	National Wildfire Coordination Group
OFT	Operational Flight Training (Leadplane)
RAO	Regional Aviation Officer
RASO	Regional Aviation Safety Officer
ROSS	Resource Ordering and Status System
SAM	State Aviation Officer (BLM)
SEAT	Single Engine Airtanker
USDA	U.S. Department of Agriculture
USFWS	U.S. Fish and Wildlife Service

Appendix A – Very Large Airtanker (VLAT) Operations

VLAT Operations

The Standard Operating Procedures listed below are to be considered when using VLAT on wildland fires. The SOPs below have made the operation with the VLAT cohesive and safe with other aerial resources.

Note: CALFIRE uses these procedures along with a flight training program. Once a Federal Leadplane Pilot is authorized to work with a VLAT, CALFIRE requires that Leadplane Pilot attend their flight training to be qualified to drop a VLAT. CALFIRE also uses a qualified ATGS in their Leadplane platform. It is highly recommended, that any Leadplane pilot from the federal government also be ASM qualified and use either an ATGS or ATS while leading the DC-10.

With VLATs being added to the compliment of conventional airtankers, measures must be taken to maximize the safety, effectiveness, and efficiency of VLAT operations. The following items need to be considered/implemented in order to mitigate the risks associated with VLAT operations.

VLAT Standard Operating Procedures

1. Establish flight paths; avoid creating hazards to other aerial resources within the FTA along with persons or property on the ground due to wake turbulence created by VLAT(s).
2. When possible, drop all conventional airtankers prior to the VLATs arrival.
3. If conventional airtanker(s) are already on scene, have them orbit above the VLAT(s) maneuvering altitude. If unable to orbit them above, then place them in a specific orbit away from the VLAT(s) IP and maneuvering area.
4. When bringing in a VLAT, you may need to orbit not only the conventional airtankers in a higher orbit, but other supervisory aircraft as well.
5. It is recommended to wait 5 minutes, but no less than 3 minutes, after the VLAT has dropped to resume conventional aerial resource operations.
6. Lead/ASM should remain on scene to perform high and low recons of the fire area. This should be done after the recommended wait time for wake turbulence. Lead will then convey air conditions over the fire area.
7. Non-essential aerial resources should be moved to an area to avoid any turbulence created by the VLAT(s). It is recommended that these same resources do not return until the 5-minute wait period.

Additional recommendation: Lead/ASM ATP pilots will be MAFFS qualified and have at least 3 full fire seasons of Leadplane experience.

DOI and FS Leadplane/ASM pilots will carry a letter of approval with them that allows them to lead VLAT's. This letter will also be retained on file with the respective national program manager(s).

This page intentionally left blank.

Appendix B - Leadplane Phase Check Oral Questions

Phase 1

1. What is the difference between an ATCO and a Leadplane pilot, and how are these positions identified in the ICS system?

2. What is the role of an ATGS over a fire and how does this position interact with the Leadplane pilot?

3. What is the role of an HLCO over a fire and how does this position interact with the Leadplane pilot?

4. What is the role of an ASM over a fire?

5. What is the role of an IC on a fire and how does this position interact with the Leadplane pilot?

6. What is the primary role of the Leadplane pilot?

7. What is the difference between the terms, required and ordered, as they relate to incident aerial supervision requirements?

8. When is Leadplane required over a fire?

9. When is an ATGS required over a fire?

10. What is the purpose of the Leadplane mentor program?

11. What are the PPE requirements while flying a Leadplane mission?

12. How often are Leadplane pilots required to attend recurrent flight and ground training?

13. What is an FTA and how does it differ from a TFR?

14. What is the standard procedure for entering and exiting the FTA for the Leadplane?

15. At what altitude do you bring the tankers into the FTA? What factors might cause you to adjust this altitude?

16. You are flying over a fire near the north end of Lake Chelan in Washington. Plot the fire location on a sectional. N 48 20 44 / W 120 43 14.

    a. What information should you look for on the sectional prior to arriving over the fire?

    b. Discuss the terrain around the fire and what conditions may exist over the fire.

    c. Discuss the airspace over the fire.

    d. What are some of your concerns about using retardant in this area?

    e. What other frequencies should you monitor?

17. What are the different types of power lines you may encounter on a fire and can you drop over or on power lines?

18. What is the safest area to cross over a set of high-tension power lines?

19. What is the minimum drop height for a large airtanker? What is the minimum drop height for a SEAT? Why do we have a minimum drop height?

20. Can you drop next to crews on the ground?

21. Describe coverage levels and how they are used.

22. Is a coverage level 4 from a P3 the same as a coverage level 4 from a P2?

23. When would you brief an inbound tanker and what information would you give them?

24. What is the purpose of a show me run?

25. Describe the information you would talk about with the airtanker on a show me run.

26. Describe ways you can join up with an airtanker.

27. During a join up who has responsibility for separation?

28. What should you do if you lost sight of an airtanker during the join up?

29. What do you do in the event of an overrun?

30. What is an IP and when would it be used?

31. Discuss mountain flying weather, terrain, and techniques.

32. What is the maximum angle of bank when exiting a run? Is there any time you can exceed this bank angle?

33. At what point during the final approach to the drop area should you start to accelerate? When should you start to clean up the aircraft?

34. What criteria should you use to evaluate a tankers drop? When should you give this evaluation?

35. What are some possible distractions a Leadplane pilot might incur while operating over a fire?

36. What are some conditions that may warrant shutting down airtanker operations?

Phase 2

1. Discuss flight following policies and options when dispatched to an incident? How does this differ in Alaska?

2. What is the transponder code that is used for firefighting aircraft? Would you use that code while en route to and from the fire?

3. Describe the differences between a variable flow, a constant flow, and a pressurized tank system.

4. List each operational airtanker type and identify its tank system.

5. Describe the variations between SEAT tank systems and their coverage patterns.

6. Discuss the individual strengths and weaknesses of SEATs and heavy airtankers while building retardant line.

7. Discuss the factors that might cause the coverage level on the ground to be different than the coverage level selected by the pilot.

8. How can you manage your radios and what should you be listening to?

9. How would you change the way you manage your radios when you are dispatched to California?

10. What should you do while en route to a fire?

11. What information should you pass on when giving a fire size up?

12. Who might you contact with a fire size up?

13. Name the locations of the large airtanker bases in each state?

14. What is the difference between a temporary and a reload base?

15. What is an example of a retardant and a suppressant and what are the differences?

16. What is the difference between fugitive and non fugitive retardant, and where might they be used?

17. What are some concerns with working helicopters and fixed wing aircraft in the same area?

18. What are some techniques in ensuring separation of helicopters and fixed wing aircraft working in the same area?

19. If you are diverted to a different fire, what information do you need to get from dispatch? What will be some of your concerns?

20. What should you do in the case of an aircraft accident or ground personnel accident?

21. Give some examples of anchor points and describe the use of them.

22. What is a tactical frequency and how is it used on a fire?

23. Describe natural fire breaks and how they are incorporated in the construction of retardant line.

24. Discuss unique hazards associated with dropping over flat terrain.

25. Describe the air and ground resources needed to control a small fire with a high rate of spread in grassy flat lands.

26. Describe the air and ground resources needed to control a small fire with a high rate of spread in mountainous terrain with heavy timber.

27. You are on final for a retardant drop and you notice crews working in the drop area that the ATGS said was clear. What do you do? What if a house was about to burn?

28. When on a base leg for a retardant drop, another tanker calls twelve miles out. What are you going to tell the inbound tanker?

29. What is considered a standard pattern for the airtanker? When would you use a non standard pattern and what might be some of your or the tanker pilots concerns for using a non standard pattern?

30. You are on final for a retardant run when the airtanker says that they have a problem.
    a. What would you do?
    b. How can you help?
    c. Should you follow the airtanker back to the tanker base?

31. A drop is made and you see it is way off target. How would you discuss it with the airtanker crew?

32. Identify some factors that influence when you would order relief.

33. Discuss how you would brief a relief Leadplane arriving over your fire.

34. What side of a fire line would you treat with retardant while supporting a burn out?

35. You are working a fire which has made a run up the slope and is approaching the ridgeline. Where would you put the retardant?

36. What problems will you have when mixing retardant drops and water drops to build line?

37. Describe the difference between a simplex and a duplex frequency for the FM radio.

38. Where would you find information for a specific airtanker base?

39. What are the advantages or disadvantages of dropping retardant into the wind, with the wind, or crosswind?

40. What are some of the difficulties and concerns when you fly a pattern that has a tail wind on base?

41. What are some issues to be aware of during downwind drops in relation to groundspeed climb gradient, etc?

42. Discuss how the different airspace around an airport might influence your operations over a fire.

43. Describe methods to maintain aircraft separation with a mix of airtankers over an incident.

44. How do you determine the minimum visibility and wind speed while over a fire?

45. Describe the difference between a fixed tank and bucket on a helicopter. How will this affect the type of dipsite they will need?

46. Discuss the tactics for a fire that is spotting out in front of the head. How would you change your tactics if there were structures threatened?

47. You have lost communications with the ground but can still talk with the airtanker. No one else in the air is having trouble communicating with the ground. Can you still make the retardant drop as planned?

48. You are on final for a live retardant run when the frequency you are using for airtanker operations suddenly becomes congested with other traffic. What should you do?

49. You notice a significant gap in the retardant load as it exits the airtanker. What could have been the cause and how might it be solved?

50. What ways could you get a quick evaluation of the drop prior to flying back over the drop?

51. What is the difference between a level 1 and a level 2 SEAT?

52. What specific authorizations do you have after taking the certificate of waiver for the Grand Canyon Park Special Flight Rules Area training?

Phase 3

1. You are over a fire with no ATGS and a media helicopter calls you wanting footage of the fire. Do you allow them over the fire? If so, at what altitude will you bring them in? Do they have the right to enter the FTA? Do they have the right to enter the TFR?

2. You are over a fire with no ATGS and a law enforcement helicopter calls you wanting to evaluate the fire. Do you allow them over the fire? If so, at what altitude will you bring them in? Do they have the right to enter the FTA? Do they have the right to enter the TFR?

3. Can general aviation aircraft come into an FTA or a TFR?

4. What should be done if you have an intrusion in the TFR? What would you do differently if there was no TFR in place?

5. You are on final with the airtanker preparing to drop a load of retardant when a ground crew calls and informs you that they are deploying their shelters and are about to get burned over. What do you do?

6. List the locations of tactical air resources, fixed wing and helicopters, in your region.

7. How do you order more air or ground resources on a fire with an ATGS on scene? With no ATGS on scene? With no ATGS or ground resources?

8. Describe a use of the guard frequency when you are over a fire with other aviation resources.

9. You, along with a jump ship and three airtankers are dispatched to a fire. You are the first aircraft on scene. The jump ship is 3 minutes out and the airtankers are 5 minutes out. Describe what you are going to do and how you are going to coordinate the air resources.

10. You are working with an ATGS on a fire. The ATGS requests that you take over air tactical duties while he goes in for fuel and lunch. Can you take over for the ATGS? If so, what information do you need to get from him prior to his departure? Who should you inform of this transfer of duties? What liabilities are you taking on?

11. What are some of the concerns with mixing large airtankers and SEATs into the same pattern over a fire?

12. What frequency should you monitor when you are flying near the Canadian border?

13. Can a US Leadplane lead a Canadian airtanker in the US?

14. Can a Canadian Bird Dog lead a US airtanker in the US?

15. At what wind speed is it generally ineffective to drop retardant?

16. What is the Grant of Exemption 392? Describe the terms and conditions of this grant of exemption.

17. What are the general differences between the flight crew duty day and flight hour policy phase 1, 2, and 3 requirements?

18. Can an ATGS direct a MAFFs aircraft for a retardant drop?

19. When are Leadplane pilots required to attend MAFFS training?

20. What are the cut off time parameters for large airtanker operations? How do the cut off times differ for single engine aircraft? How do the cut off times differ for aircraft in Alaska?

21. You have 5 airtankers over a fire and they are all released back to the tanker base due to excessive wind over the fire. How should you release them back to the base? What factors will you take into consideration?

Appendix C – ATGS Refresher Training Exercise

The Goal of the ATGS refresher training exercise is to ensure the safety of aviation operations is retained as it pertains to the ATGS position.

The ATGS will demonstrate the following fundamental ATGS skills:

- FTA entry
- Determine and assign FTA altitudes for incoming aircraft
- Initial aircraft briefings
- Maintain vertical and horizontal aircraft separation
- Communication with air and ground resources
- Situational awareness

The exercise will be evaluated by an ATGS (C) utilizing the Aerial Supervision Mission Evaluation form.

Exercise objective: Demonstrate fundamental ATGS skills within 15 minutes.

Exercise elements and role players:

- Initial attack fire with the following resources:
    - On scene:
        - IC
        - One engine crew
        - One hand crew
    - Enroute:
        - 2 helicopters
        - 2 airtankers
    - Dispatch

Exercise sequence:

1. ATGS receives aircraft dispatch form with resource information and altimeter setting
2. ATGS launches from home base and establishes contact with dispatch.
3. ATGS initiates FTA entry procedures 12 miles from incident
4. ATGS arrives on scene, makes contact with IC and establishes objectives and priorities. Fire elevation is indicated on sand table.
5. Enroute aircraft (airtankers and helicopters) check in at 12 miles.
6. ATGS provides initial briefing.
7. Aircraft arrive on scene; ATGS provides tactical briefing based on incident objectives.
8. ATGS coordinates helicopter work and retardant drops.
9. ATGS ensures line clearance during helicopter and airtanker operations.
10. ATGS solicits feedback from IC regarding helicopter and airtanker operations.

11. ATGS gives departure briefing or additional instructions to airtankers and helicopters.
12. End of exercise.

Exercise conclusion: ATGS and evaluator debrief utilizing the Aerial Supervision Mission Evaluation.

Appendix D – Aerial Supervision Mission Checklist

Aircraft Mission Checklist

Aerial Supervision

Pre-Flight

- Mission fuel   Confirmed
- Weather enroute/destination   Checked
- Resource order/mission brief   Accomplished
- Standard aircraft brief   Accomplished

After Takeoff/Enroute

- GPS   Set
- Communication/radios   Confirmed/set
- Other aircraft on scene/enroute   Confirmed
- Level of supervision on scene   Confirmed
- Alternate airport(s)   Confirmed
- Time on station (Bingo)   Determined **/Re evaluate***
- Crew brief   Accomplished

Prior to FTA entry

- Altimeter   Set
- Pulse/ landing lights   On
- Transponder   On/ALT

* In the event of divert to a new incident, checklist items after "Pre-Flight" will be re-done.

This page intentionally left blank.

Appendix E – Fire Traffic Area Card

Fire Traffic Area (FTA)   01 May 2013

*** Clearance is required to enter the FTA ***

Initial Radio Contact: 12 nm on assigned air tactical frequency.
No Radio Contact: Hold a minimum of 7 nm from the incident.

Note: Airtanker maneuvering altitude determines minimum airtanker and ATGS orbit altitudes. Assigned altitudes may be higher and will be stated as MSL.

Media
VFR *

Note 1

ATGS Orbit	2500' AGL Minimum

Note 2

1500' AGL Minimum	Airtanker Orbit

Note 2

Airtanker Maneuvering	Maximum 1000' AGL

Max 500' AGL	Helicopters *

SFC   SFC

| 12nm | 7nm | 5nm | 0 | 5nm | 7nm | 12nm |

Note 3   Note 3

Note 1	1000' min. separation between ATGS orbit and airtanker orbit altitude.
Note 2	500' min. separation between airtanker orbit and maneuvering altitude.
Note 3	On arrival reduce speed to cross 7 nm at assigned altitude and 150 KIAS or less.

* Helicopters: Fly assigned altitudes and routes.

* Media: Maintain VFR separation above highest incident aircraft or position and altitude as assigned by controlling aircraft.

Airtanker Base As Assigned	Air Guard 168.625 Tx Tone 110.9	Air To Air As Assigned	National Flight Following 168.650 Tone 110.9 TX and RX

National Interagency Airspace: http://airspacecoordination.org

Incident Airspace Reminders

Fire Traffic Area (FTA)

- The FTA is a communication protocol for firefighting agencies. It does not pertain to other aircraft that have legal access granted by the FAA within a specific TFR.
- The FTA should not be confused with a TFR, which is a legal restriction established by the Federal Aviation Administration to restrict aviation traffic while the other is a communication tool establishing protocol within firefighting agencies.
  - Participating aircraft must adhere to TFR policies as established by the FAA.
  - For example, if the TFR boundary of a polygon exceeds the 12-mile initial contact ring, clearance will still be required in order to enter the TFR.
  - If the TFR boundary is within the 12-mile ring, proceed with standard FTA communication procedures.

Temporary Flight Restriction (TFR)

- All assigned/ordered aircraft must obtain clearance into or the incident TFR by the on scene aerial supervision or the official in charge of the on-scene emergency response activities.
- Aircraft not assigned to the incident must stay clear the TFR unless communication is established with the controlling entity (ATGS, ASM, Leadplane, etc.) and authorization is given to enter/transit the TFR.
- The first responding aircraft, typically on extended attack incidents, must have reasonable assurance that there are no other aircraft in the TFR by making blind calls on the TFR frequency and double checking with ground personnel (IC, OPS, or Helibase).
- There may be multiple aircraft operations areas within a single TFR.
- Remember - Non-Incident aircraft may enter the TFR under the following conditions:
  - The aircraft is carrying **law enforcement** officials.
  - The aircraft is carrying **properly accredited news representatives.**
  - The aircraft is operating under the **ATC approved IFR flight plan.**
  - The operation is conducted **directly to or from an airport** within the area, or is necessitated by the impracticability of VFR flight above or around the area due to weather, or terrain; notification is given to the Flight Service Station (FSS) or **ATC facility** specified in the NOTAM to receive advisories concerning disaster relief aircraft operations; and the operation does not hamper or endanger relief activities and is not conducted for observing the disaster.
- **A ROSS order or Aircraft Dispatch Form is not a clearance into a TFR.**

Further Information: *Interagency Aerial Supervision Guide*, PMS 505

User Notes

Notes:

Notes:

Notes: